SAVE OUR SISTERS

Morgan Barney

McCall Barney

Brianna Copeland

Elise Griffin

Kristie Watkins

Maleah Weir

DEDICATION

To all the abolitionists

CONTENTS

ACKNOWLEDGMENTS

A special thank you to all of our parents for the endless support, car rides, food, prayer, wisdom, and hospitality;

To our brothers and sisters who are faithfully present with helping hands;

To the families that support us financially, with much kindness and encouragement;

To our church and pastoral staff for unwavering support and belief in God's work through the youth;

To the churches, radio stations, conferences, and small groups that have hosted us and been a part of our story;

To the organizations fighting for freedom around the globe—walking in justice, righteousness, and shalom;

To all the individuals reading this book, thank you.

All to Christ—

FOREWORD

Over the years I have travelled to many churches, conferences, and campuses as an itinerant minister. Along the way, I have met interesting people of all ages and backgrounds, each with his or her own unique story. In particular, I love to hear of the young people who do not wait until adulthood to turn their passion for God into ministry. As I meet remarkable young people I like to share their journey with others as well. This is where the women of SOS come into the story.

Matt Capps, a former student who has continued as a ministry friend, asked me to speak at Calvary Baptist Church's West Campus in Winston-Salem, North Carolina one Wednesday night. He missed that night because he was travelling overseas to adopt a precious child. I spoke on a theme dear to my heart: reaching the next generation. After the service a young lady came to meet me and to tell me a little of her story. Her name is Morgan, and she was 14 at the time. What a beautiful irony that the very night my host was gone to adopt a child, I met some young ladies hoping to rescue many more.

Over the next few years I worked with these young ladies in several events at my church, on campus at Southeastern Baptist Theological Seminary, and the Baptist State Convention of North Carolina's State Evangelism Conference. I grew to love these young women and the hearts they have for Christ and for the broken. More recently, I had Brianna (and her husband, Travis!) in class at the College of Southeastern. I have watched these young ladies grow into adults and seen their ministry expand. This is a story worth knowing, telling, and supporting.

What you will read in the following pages is the story of Morgan, Brianna, Maleah, McCall, Kristie, and Elise, all part of the ministry they call SOS (Save Our Sisters, www.saveoursisterstoday.com). These women, along with many in their generation, stand in solidarity with young women in other lands who live under the bondage of slavery. The most recent data reveals that there are more than 45.8 million people enslaved.[1] Not only are these people enslaved, but many live under the fist of the most sinister example of slavery: sex trafficking.

The following pages have a twofold purpose. First, the ladies of SOS want to inform you of the reality of the plight of their sisters in places across the world, including the United States. You will read real stories and the latest statistics on this evil. But make no mistake, although they are young, the SOS women understand the greatest bondage is to sin. The ultimate goal is to set the captives free so they can hear about the love of a redeeming Savior.

The second purpose of this book is to tell the specific story of the ministry of SOS, particularly their role in Moldova, and their ministry of spreading the message of freedom in the gospel. Any donations these young women receive, including profit from the sale of this book, will go directly to their ministry to fight sex trafficking in Moldova and to raise awareness about the issue in America.

I urge you to read this book, order copies for as many people as you can, and help spread the good news of Jesus in the face of real evil.

Alvin L. Reid
Senior Professor of Evangelism and Student Ministry and Bailey Smith Chair of Evangelism at Southeastern Baptist Theological Seminary

INTRODUCTION

While I was studying for ministry at Southeastern Baptist Theological Seminary, I enrolled in an evangelism course with Dr. Alvin Reid. In one of the lectures, Dr. Reid walked through the history of the church and highlighted the work of young people in spiritual movements from Pietism, to the First and Second Great Awakening, to the Welsh Revivals, to the Jesus Movement, and many others. There was one common thread, namely, God using young people in a mighty way. Students are perhaps the most fertile field for the working of the Spirit of God. However, in our culture and in our churches, it is far too common to expect little out of our young people. It's happening all around us, young people taking longer to reach adulthood and more importantly, struggling to find meaningful purpose in life, much less a way to make a difference in our world.

Thankfully there are exceptions to this sad cultural

phenomenon. There are young people who are resolved, as John Piper has notably proclaimed, to "not waste their lives."[1] The young women who are behind the movement of Save Our Sisters are a great example. While I served as one of the pastors at Calvary Baptist Church in Winston-Salem, North Carolina, I had the privilege of watching McCall, Morgan, Kristie, Elise, Brianna and Maleah grow and take action as the Lord grasped their hearts by the power of the gospel, encouraging them to shine its freeing light in the dark and enslaving realm of human trafficking.

Our world is abounding with the sad implications of sin, and the millions of people enslaved in sex trafficking is a gut-wrenching example of this. Thankfully, these young women have fallen on their faces before God and set their hands to the plow to join God on his mission to set the captives free. I could not be more thrilled to see their story in print. Not only will you be encouraged and educated by what you read here, you will also be profoundly challenged. The Bible is clear that our God is a missionary God. God is working towards redeeming and restoring all things and individuals.

Certainly, the gospel is central to all of our mission endeavors. Our mission flows out of the gospel. These young women understand that we are a missionary people reflecting a missionary God. Throughout these pages you will see a clear example of gospel driven mission, a call to "seek the welfare of the city" (Jeremiah 29:7). As Jesus said in Matthew 5:14-16, "You are the light of the world…let your light shine before others, so that they may see your good works and give glory to your Father who is in heaven."

My prayer is that those who read these pages will be challenged to raise the bar in their own lives, but also encourage young people around them to do the same by shining the light of the gospel in the darkest places. To God be the glory for these young women, their story, and how it will be used to light a fire in those who read it.

Rev. Matt Capps
Senior Pastor,
Fairview Baptist Church in Apex, North Carolina

1

The Slave trade

"He has delivered us from the domain of darkness and transferred us to the kingdom of his beloved Son."
Colossians 1:13

Identity in a Name

Think for a moment about your name—your full name. Imagine the joy of your parents the day you were born, giving you a name. Picture those first moments when you were called by your name and when you first responded with understanding to its uniqueness.

Our names range from common to unique: Morgan, Brianna, Maleah, McCall, Kristie, and Elise. Whether your name is uncommon or well known, your name is a symbol of your worth. Your name tells you that you are not a number; you are more than a generic cog in the system — you are a person. You know your name, and your name is known by the God who created you.

Now, imagine you are a 16-year-old girl raised in a cold Moldovan orphanage. The singular possession that belongs to you is your name, Natasha. As an infant, your mother abandoned you to the mercies of an orphanage, and you have been raised in this life ever since. All your life you have fought for survival: struggling for food, fighting for a warm place to sleep, and warding off the older boys in the orphanage from taking advantage of you.

Suddenly a glimmer of hope shines in your seemingly destitute existence. The time has come for your release from the clutches of the orphanage. Finally, freedom from this dark place.

Or so you think.

With a mere glance, the orphanage director hands you forty dollars and a bus ticket.[1] You are excited, but uncertain of what to expect from an unknown society. It seems like a dream at first. A fresh start, a clean slate, a chance to begin again.

When you step off the bus, a man approaches you eagerly. He smiles slyly, strangely captivating you with his unfamiliar friendliness. He compliments you, admiring your crystal blue eyes and flaxen hair. He promises that you would be just the right girl for his latest job opportunity.

Since you know no one and have no place to stay, you decide to accept his enchanting offer. He seems to care about you, and he exhibits a confidence you have never seen before. After a short bus ride, you are sitting in his home, marveling at your good fortune. But soon the mask of kindness slips away as his promises begin to reveal their emptiness.

After a few minutes of silence, he speaks up. "You naïve little girl," he says harshly, "you belong to me now. Your name is no longer Natasha. You are mine. You will now be called number 189."

The dream you imagined immediately changes into a nightmarish reality. A fog slowly settles over you, the result of the drugs he slipped into your tea earlier. Then, he drags you into the upper level of the house where a number of other girls—half-clothed and as thin as rails— stumble around in a similar daze.

Goodbye Natasha. Say hello to the world of human trafficking. You are now known as number 189. You represent another victim of the sex-slave trade.

A Modern-Day Nightmare

While this story may seem unrealistic and overly grotesque, it represents the plight of millions of women and children around the globe. Approximately 5.5 million children lose their childhood to sexual exploitation and enslavement each year.[2] This includes victims of the international crime of modern-day sex-slavery, also known as human sex trafficking. Sex trafficking is one of the most common types of human trafficking, while other types of trafficking include forced labor and debt bondage. These precious children have their entire childhood stripped away. Any memories of innocence and vitality are replaced with abuse and violence. Enslaved children never get to enjoy sunny days, play with their friends, or even go to school. This developmentally critical time period for growing kids is completely disregarded.

Joy forgotten.

Happiness lost.

Freedom stolen.

Practically every sort of evil is wrapped into this one ever-growing crime called human trafficking: coercion, fraud, selfishness, identity theft, murder, rape, money laundering, greed, kidnapping, illegal weaponry and drug trade. An official definition outlines this nightmare by explaining:

> 'Trafficking in persons' and 'human trafficking' have been used as umbrella terms for the act of recruiting, harboring, transporting, providing, or obtaining persons for compelled labor or commercial sex acts through the use of force, fraud, or coercion.[3]

We often live in denial when subjects like this arise. Ugliness hurts, and our natural tendency is to choose to ignore pain, to avoid truth, and shove away harsh realities.

However, we cannot be silent while so many young people are exploited. When Save Our Sisters began, there were over 27 million slaves worldwide, more than ever before in the course of human history. [4] Yet today, the most recent data is estimating that there are more than 45.8 million people enslaved.[5] Wrestling with the fact that our world enslaves more people now than the entire duration of the African Slave Trade seems unimaginable. During the African Slave Trade, slavery was legal and promoted. Now, slavery is illegal in most countries, yet more prominent than we dare to believe.

The modern day sex trade has risen from the ashes of an issue many thought to be long gone. With the abolition of the legal slave trade in Britain in 1833, and the abolition of the African Slave Trade in the United States in 1865, many believe slavery is a thing of the past. However, this lucrative trade of persons has not ceased to exist. The development of the internet, the ease of border transport from agreements like NATO (North Atlantic Treaty Organization) and the EU (European Union), and the sexual revolution that has swept the Western hemisphere since the early 1960s have created an ideal environment to advance this international crime.

Every minute, two children are prepared for sexual exploitation.[6]

Every thirty seconds—the time it takes to order food from the drive through—a child is abused.

This statistic should break your heart. Women and

children stuck in the bondage of sexual exploitation have been manipulated into thinking the life they live is normal and even acceptable. For some, this forced existence is all they have ever known. We have heard multiple stories of little children growing up under the bed of slavery. Anika is one of them. She was born in the sex-traffick-ridden city of Calcutta, India. Her mother gave birth to her amongst the disease-infested filth of her brothel stall. Her mother was forced to continue her work as a sex-slave while attempting to raise her child. To quiet and calm the baby while her mother worked with customers, she was encouraged to feed Anika alcohol. Thankfully, this little one escaped the clutches of trafficking and now lives in the loving care of a safe home—a place where she can heal, experience holistic rehabilitation, and know what real love is like. However, her kidneys suffered damage from the alcohol, and her life bears the scars of bondage.

Victims of sex trafficking can be men or women, girls or boys, but the majority are women and girls.[7] There are a number of common patterns for luring victims into situations of sex trafficking, including:

- The promise of a good job
- A false marriage proposal
- Threats against the victims and victim's family

Trafficking Schemes

Sex traffickers frequently subject their victims to debt-bondage: an illegal practice in which traffickers convince their victims that they owe them money and must work to pay them back in order to earn their freedom. They trick the girls into believing any living expenses or transportation costs to the new city are the girls' responsibility. As a result, they must pledge their sexual services to repay the debt. All the while, as the victims are working to pay off the debt, the traffickers provide shelter, clothing, and sometimes food for girls which they will add to their debt bondage total, making it virtually impossible for girls to gain their freedom from this cyclical trap.

Sex traffickers use a variety of methods to "condition" their victims. These include but are not limited to starvation, confinement, beating, physical abuse, rape, gang rape, threats of violence against the victims and their families, forced drug use, and threats of shame by revealing their activities.

The psychological effects of this lifestyle are as devastating as the physical conditions. Popular psychological harms include shame, grief, fear, distrust, hatred of men, self-hatred, suicidal thoughts and suicidal actions. Victims are at risk for Post-Traumatic Stress Disorder (PTSD), which is displayed by symptoms of acute anxiety, depression, insomnia, and physical hyper alertness. It is common for victims to suffer from trauma bonding—a form of coercive control in which the perpetrator instills fear in the victim as well as gratitude for being allowed to live, which causes a false dependence and attachment to the trafficker. Trauma bonding commonly manifests itself when a girl is trafficked by her former 'boyfriend'. This occurs when a victim believes she is actually loved by this 'boyfriend' and shows him love by preforming the sex acts he asks for, and also servicing his friends. This is one of the most devastating factors affecting trafficking victims because the psychological damage remains long after they are removed from a harmful situation. Undoing the deeply embedded psychological consequences of trauma bonding is some of the hardest work of rehabilitation for those who survive a trafficking experience.

A Global Pandemic

Human trafficking rivals the illicit drug trade as the number one international crime.[8] Unlike drugs, women can be sold and resold. You can use a drug once and the deal is done. A woman, however, can be sold and raped repeatedly, bringing in more money as a valuable asset. In the business world of infraction, "pimping out" girls is completely rational. Women are a renewable product, sold up to 30 times a day,[9] and bringing in an average revenue of $150,000 per year, per victim.[10] A trafficker with a ring of just ten girls would make an enormous profit annually.

The drive for money and continual striving for more fuels the endless, lucrative commerce. Human trafficking revenue tips the scales at a staggering $99 billion dollars, an annual income higher than that of Apple ($46 billion), Nike ($30 billion), and Starbucks ($21 billion) combined.[11]

It's obvious that this industry is riddled with every sort of evil. If this is true, why is it still an issue? Scripture tells us that the love of money is a root of all sorts of evil, and the progressive greed of human nature is what perpetuates the endless cycle of sin.

> For the love of money is a root of all kinds of evils. It is through this craving that some have wandered away from the faith and pierced themselves with many pangs.
>
> 1 Timothy 6:10

This desire for money is the root of the supply and demand cycle. With money as a functional savior, some will even go to the lengths of selling humans to fill their deepest desires. Money promises power, security, and control. These illusive promises drive many to value money more than human life—especially the lives of the vulnerable. Valuing money and gain over the lives of people finds its end in this: the very industry of human trafficking.

Allow these facts of slavery to resonate in your heart and mind. Grapple with it, wrestle a while, and talk about it with others—whether that be parents, friends, a group at church, or a spouse. Before you read the rest of this book, please stop and pray for the international industry of sex trafficking to be broken by the freedom of the gospel, one life at a time.

We can write with the most descriptive language and seek to eloquently convey the stories of human trafficking victims, but the reality of the situation is something we will never, ever quite understand. This story is more than just the retelling of a humanitarian effort, it is about the condition of the human heart. This means that the solution to the problem must be more than just a humanitarian answer: the solution must be Christ.

Throughout the rest of the pages, we hope that you will share in what the Lord has taught us. We are nothing special. In fact, we are sometimes quite clueless and so imperfect. But Christ is the author of this story, and he deserves all glory.

Let's begin.

2

The Story of Save Our Sisters

"So, whether you eat or drink, or whatever
you do, do it all for the glory of God."
1 Corinthians 10:31

The Beginning

The ministry of Save Our Sisters (SOS) emerged the summer of 2010, but its beginning reaches back two years prior when we were in middle school, when our friendships first began to form. Our passion for the ministry of SOS has been slowly cultivated our entire lives. Six individual girls drawn from four families compose the SOS leadership team.

We—Brianna, Morgan, McCall, Maleah, Kristie and Elise—are all extremely blessed to have been raised in

Christian homes where our parents instilled in us the desire to obey God and serve others. As young girls, we were constantly taught the significance of protecting our purity as a way to love and honor God. It became a concept used in our everyday conversation. We learned that our hearts, minds, and bodies belong to God. He created us in his image, to love him as our Lord and Maker, and we wanted to honor him in everything we did. The importance of keeping his intentions for marriage and personal purity resonated deeply inside our middle school minds where boys were often a hot topic. As children of God, we sought to understand our responsibility to keep ourselves pure as a way of worshipping the Lord.

In 2008, when we were in sixth and seventh grade, a couple of our moms led us through the *Lies Young Women Believe* Bible study by Nancy Leigh DeMoss and Dannah Gresh.[1] This initial Bible study sparked in us a hunger for the Word and for delving into the riches of Scripture in community with others. We centered our growing friendships around loving Jesus and knowing him by continuing Bible studies on our own and keeping one another accountable.

Fast forward to July 4th, 2010, Independence Day. The eighth grade girls Bible Fellowship class sat in a prayer room on a Sunday morning at Calvary Baptist Church in Winston Salem, North Carolina. Given the holiday, we discussed our various freedoms that morning in our Sunday school class. Out of the blue—to this day we still have only the Holy Spirit to credit—Morgan said she was thankful she was not physically enslaved like so many young girls in the world.

Little did we know, this one statement would change the trajectory of our lives.

Morgan began to elaborate on the topic of human trafficking, informing us there are more slaves today than ever before in history. She shared how this issue is prominent all around the world, how girls are treated like property instead of people, and how some girls as young as five years old are forced to perform daily sex acts. The demand for younger girls has replaced the demand for women by more than 11% in the last fifteen years.[2] The list of statistics seemed to never end. With each new fact she shared about the reality of this atrocity, our tender hearts were broken to pieces.

As we mentioned, throughout middle school much time and instruction was focused on our own purity and God's design for intimacy. This became a mission for us, to save the sacred gift of sex for marriage. We were ready to keep each other accountable and encouraged. When we learned that girls around the globe have their personal innocence stripped away from them every day, it was particularly difficult for us to fathom.

It took us a few months after SOS began to trace this correlation to our desire for purity. We found ourselves wondering why we had such an interest in sexual slavery— why not something like world hunger? Human trafficking is such a dark and evil issue. At first, our parents were skeptical of their 14-year-old daughters and our younger sisters researching and involving ourselves in the fight against this global nightmare. During our season of research, our parents knew all about what we were learning and they helped us process the reality of evil with the triumph of truth. They have been deeply involved in the process of Save Our Sisters since day one. It was obvious that God heightened our awareness and burdened our hearts for this specific avenue of justice, and we knew we were called to act.

The Sleepover

There is one thing teenage girls do better than anyone else — sleepovers! Little did we know that a ministry could be born out of a simple slumber party. After approving the plans for the evening with our parents, this night started like any other sleepover, soaking up the last of summer before our first year of high school began. We felt so old and scared. We felt like our lives were moving forward too fast. We promised each other that we would make the next four years count. We did not want to walk across the stage on graduation day and wonder what our high school years could have been, we did not want to be left with any "what-ifs." Our simple cry was to make God known and to make a difference, no matter how small.

The topic of sex slavery from the prior Independence

Sunday quickly made its way into our conversation. The struggle between empathy and compassion ached in our hearts. Should we try to do something? What could we do? We were only twelve and fourteen years old! There was a certain anticipation that fell on us. Our minds were racing and hearts heavy with a burden for the lost and hurting. We wanted to do more than feel bad for girls in bondage. We wanted to do something.

Our conversation quickly turned to action. We began throwing out all kinds of crazy ideas, undying hopes, and limitless dreams. When we stopped for a second to catch our breath and calm down, we realized that maybe some of these ideas could actually occur! We sat on the bedroom floor stunned at the rapid turn of events. Through our energetic frenzy, we landed on the idea of having a cookout with our youth group.

Within minutes we began spitting out names for this cookout. Most were too alliterative and cheesy to stick (we were fourteen-year-old girls, remember?). But one would not escape our minds: Save Our Sisters.

Immediately Isaiah 61 came to mind, as we had been memorizing this passage together over the summer. We quickly grabbed a Bible to confirm our mission. Isaiah 61 reads,

> The Spirit of the sovereign Lord is upon me, because the Lord has anointed me to preach good news to the poor. He has sent me to bind up the broken hearted, to proclaim freedom for

the captives, and release from darkness for the prisoners, to bestow on them a crown of beauty instead of ashes.

Isaiah 61:1 and 3 [NIV]

With this scripture, God reassured us we were exactly where he wanted us to be, fulfilling the work he had prepared for us in Christ Jesus, before the foundation of the world (Ephesians 1:4). The power of the Holy Spirit in a ninth grader's bedroom on that particular summer night was undeniable.

The Big Event

Resulting from the flurry of brainstorm ideas at the sleepover, a student-wide cookout on the soccer field at our church was soon in the works. We lined up a couple meetings with leaders in our church and we were eager to testify to all the ways in which God was revealing himself to us. They supported us with wisdom and insight, steering our untamed passion into a focused effort. Research and statistics soon began filling our days. We realized we knew hardly anything about the issue of human trafficking, and to our surprise, neither did the adults around us. Why did no one know about this problem? Why was no one talking about it? We were hungry for stories, knowledge, and understanding of this social injustice. We made a list of potential ministries to donate the money we hoped to raise and in our research we discovered Project Rescue. Project Rescue is an incredible organization that runs holistic safe homes for survivors in India, Nepal, Bangledesh, Moldova, Tajikistan, Spain, and France.[3] The International Justice Mission also serves tirelessly to bring criminals to justice, rescue victims, restore survivors, and strengthen governmental justice systems.[4] Project Rescue and the International Justice Mission are excellent organizations doing great work and we decided the money we raised from our first cookout would support these ministries.

In the coming weeks, we promoted our event on local radio stations, posted flyers all over town, and spread the word to anyone who would share in our excitement. Local stores and bakeries donated food, cakes, gift certificates, and supplies. We were amazed by the support we received. It felt like a true community effort. Planning this event was definitely a learning curve—we had never before processed the concept of needing not only the food, but the table for the food, the tablecloth for the table, a grill master for the burgers, and silverware to dish out the baked beans. We pulled together over thirty committed volunteers, food for five-hundred people, and a soccer field full of fun.

After much planning, many meetings, and detailed preparation, mid-September arrived, and it was the night of our cook out. The night was full: including a live band, tables lined with information, brochures, custom T-shirts, prayer stations with statistics from countries all over the world, and stories of lives torn apart by trafficking.

We tried not to hold any expectations for the night because quite honestly, we had no idea what to even expect! To our astonishment, well over five-hundred guests joined us that evening including friends and family, members of adult Bible Fellowship classes, and youth groups from across our city came to learn and act as abolitionists.

Everything exceeded our wildest dreams! In the middle of the evening, we paused for a time of guided prayer. Guests were instructed to walk from station to station learning about how trafficking expressed itself in specific countries around the world. Several missionaries joined this prayer station endeavor by sharing their experiences and leading prayer. Morgan and McCall's Aunt Linda traveled two hours from Raleigh to share about the country of Moldova. Originally, we only included Moldova as a means to simply cover the European region and share another facet of trafficking. Little did we know this seemingly insignificant country would fuel our passion and shape our ministry in the coming months.

Aunt Linda came equipped with a smile and sunflowers to decorate the station. She also brought a very special guest—Irina, a teenage girl visiting from Moldova. Irina blessed us with her kind spirit and love for the Lord. Through her thick Romanian accent, Irina shared of her life in Moldova and the realities of trafficking all around her. The Lord was preparing our hearts through this unexpected friendship to eventually fall in love with the country of Moldova.

During the time of prayer we walked out on the field and felt the overwhelming power of the Holy Spirit at work. It was in that moment the ministry of Save Our Sisters was confirmed in the depths of our beings. This was going to be more than a one-time event. Christ was calling us to more!

Life Begins At The End of Your Comfort Zone

This ministry isn't about us. It never has been. Our dream dawned late summer of 2010, and we never imagined the journey Christ had prepared for us. If someone would have told us where we would be now, we would have never believed them (Habakkuk 1:5). We had no idea we would be given the opportunity to raise funds, build a safe house in Moldova, rescue girls from slavery, and to share the love of Christ with survivors. Our core leadership team has fluctuated throughout times of refinement. We have learned a lot about working with close friends and people you love. It is not always easy. God has knit together a group of six best friends, despite our differences. Five of us were homeschooled, one went to a public high school, and now we are all at different colleges in three different states! We come from different families with different stories, but we have one common goal that unites us: the glory of Christ.

We are simply another example of Christ-followers who take his Great Commission seriously, to take the gospel to the nations. We want to take the gospel to the broken. To preach good news that sets captives free, just like Jesus did (Luke 4:16-22). We long to see these victims rescued from slavery both physically and spiritually by believing in Jesus, who can set them free for all eternity.

Kristie's Story:

You may find yourself with the same misconception I often did. "These girls were homeschooled, they had time for this sort of thing." As much as I wanted to blame school, we all live busy lives. I am the only one of us that was not homeschooled, and I regularly felt this frustration. On top of going to public school, I also held a part-time job, served on the drum line at my school, and stayed involved in my youth group. It is safe to say none of us had an abundance of free time. Managing my participation in SOS has been stressful at times. When I came home from seven hours of school and then had to go to a meeting, only to go home and do three more hours of homework, it made me question my involvement. When we had opportunities to go and share at different places in high school, I often could not go because it was during the school day. That always made me wonder if it was worth it for me to be involved. When I had the most stressful and busy week and wanted nothing more than to spend Saturday relaxing at home but instead we travelled two hours for a conference, Satan tried to put excuses in my head. Yet when I take a step back and stop sulking in my never-ending list of responsibilities, I remember this life is not about me! When I stop worrying about my time, I am reminded that God does not call us to live comfortable lives where we get eight hours of sleep and have relaxing weekends. God calls us to live a life serving him and giving ourselves as a living sacrifice (Romans 12:1). I have seen time and time again in certain situations where I have been hesitant to participate because of time, God has blessed those experiences and multiplied my time, allowing me to do all I needed to do. I understand more than anyone the reasons to sit back and go through the motions. I have been there. Many times I still am, but I have to examine those reasons, look to God and what he is calling me to, and try to imagine the end result like he sees. As stressful and hectic as our lives can get, there is a more powerful sense of rest when you take a deep breath and allow God to work through you the way he intended. That rest will be more satisfying than a full night's sleep and a lazy Saturday. The eternal reward that comes from that kind of abandonment and service are worth every hour you have to add to the list of responsibilities that seem to never end. Trust me.

Remember

After our first fundraising event, we realized the work of ministry would take a lot of prayer and giving up our current lives to live in radical abandonment to Christ. Our priorities had shifted. We could no longer sit around as teenagers going through the Christian motions because Christ called us to more.

God has taught us much about how to love. He has shown us the simple things of seeking first his kingdom and righteousness, to love Jesus and love others, even when it is hard and we fail. And yes, even when it is uncomfortable. When his timing intercepts our daily me-centered plans and we want to label divine appointments as interruptions to our lives, we realize we are not just called to fight sexual slavery. We are also called to constantly fight slavery to ourselves, to what culture tells us, to our calendars, and to everything else vying for our attention.

This makes us uncomfortable.

Sacrifice makes us uncomfortable.

Scripture makes it clear that to be like Christ, we must follow him unto death. We must sacrifice as he sacrificed. It is expected of Christians that we sacrifice for the sake of Christ. Sacrifice can look like a lot of different things, maybe it means giving up that unneeded latte. Maybe it means selling your house to live in a smaller one. Maybe it means moving to a third-world country. We were not placed on this earth to live radically for Jesus for one week at summer camp or for a weekend at a worship conference and then return to our normal self-centered lives.

We so easily forget. We forget God—forget his goodness to us in the past and his promise of faithfulness to us in the future—and live as though he does not even exist. When we forget God, we also forget those he loves. In Galatians 2:10, Paul relays a message from the Apostles, saying that all they asked was for us "to remember the poor." Simply remember. We need to be reminded to remember. Remember to pray, to act, to love, and to care.

What we remember is what we value. We remember to check our phones, pay our bills, do our homework, and go about our days. But the poor? Really? Those "less fortunate" do not always top the chart of our memory and action. When we realize that we are the poor in spirit, we remember those in physical poverty around us. We must wake up and remember. Christ is good, and Christ is here, now, with us.

We are called to live radically every day, saturating it with more of Jesus and less of us. Every day, we encounter opportunities to proclaim Jesus. Every day, we encounter opportunities to walk in justice. Do not let the chance that God has given you to love him and sacrifice for him slip by, but count it as joy! Living radically requires every moment of our lives to be lived for Jesus, to be uncomfortably beautiful.

Remember Jesus, and do not be afraid of sacrifice.

3

Slavery in Moldova

The Spirit of the LORD God is upon me, because
the LORD has anointed me to bring good news
to the poor; He has sent me to bind up the
brokenhearted, to proclaim liberty to the
captives, and the opening of the prison to those
who are bound."
Isaiah 61:1

Moldova

Many do not know the location of this tiny country,
much less its hidden horrors. Landlocked between
Romania and Ukraine, Moldova seems insignificant in
comparison to the rest of the world. Home to only four
million people, Moldovan culture spans from fast-paced
city dwellers to shepherds herding sheep in the

countryside.[1] Economic depression taints the spirit of community throughout this post-communist society, making it the poorest country in Europe.[2] In addition to the oppressive nature of poverty, human trafficking has clutched this tiny nation.

Nearly one third of all Moldovans are vulnerable to being trapped, trafficked, and exploited across Europe.[3] Estimates say that over 40,000 women have been trafficked from the southern city of Cahul in the last ten years alone, some without even a trace left behind.[4] Although this is largely undocumented because of the illegal nature of the transport, it is widely believed that women serve as Moldova's number one export.

Read that again. The number one export of Moldova is believed to be trafficked women—

Not Moldova's sunflower seeds, or outsourced jobs, or even illegal weaponry.

Women.

Women and girls are lured into this trade in a variety of ways. The prospect of a job or source of income entices these vulnerable women more than anything else. Flyers advertising such jobs line the streets of Moldova, posted on telephone poles and power lines, building walls and community bulletin boards. Girls all too willingly fall for these offers, locking them into the horrid reality of sex-slavery once they arrive.

The cunning schemes of traffickers, paired with the poverty-stricken culture of Moldova, create a perfect environment for this crime. Moldova only recently gained its independence in the 1990s,[5] but Russia still holds a tight grasp on the struggling nation. Once a thriving agricultural society, Moldova now struggles with long seasons of drought, along with outdated agricultural technology.

On top of a failing economy, the family structure of Moldova is generationally gapped, where many have never experienced a home with both parents present throughout childhood. Most Moldovan fathers are completely absent from the lives of their children because of their need to find work. This presents the opportunity for younger boys to take advantage of girls and for girls to live lives of codependent helplessness. If the father is present in the lives of the children, he will most likely leave the country in search of an outsourced job, and many times so will the mother.[6] This makes for a society full of parentless children, adding to the already prominent orphan culture. There are over 13,500 children institutionalized in Moldovan orphanages. Many have no relatives, no family, and no hope. Some are there because their families simply cannot afford to keep them.[7]

The most tragic reality of this culture is the death of Christianity. As a country, Moldova has been described as a post-Christian nation, in which Christianity seems to have run its course. Those who choose to participate in any sort of religion generally fall into the Russian Orthodox tradition. Characterized by good works, indulgences, and worship of icons, the Russian Orthodox Church in Moldova often shows resistance against the gospel and against outreach to the destitute of their society. However, due to the hopelessness of the country, Moldova is a ripe harvest field for the gospel and the country is in need of willing harvest workers (Matthew 9:35-38). When the gospel is preached, the Lord saves. Consider joining a team travelling to Moldova for Moldova Mission summer camps and watch the Lord transform this country one believer at a time (www.moldovamission.com).

The Broken Fabric

What we observe in Moldova is a broken fabric. The perfect tapestry that God put in place for this world has now become completely ruined by the stain of sin. Though God made an amazing world filled with beauty and wonder, and made us in his image, sin has ravaged this world. This is why Jesus came, lived, and died for us— to offer hope to the hopeless. His death and resurrection have overcome the world (John 16:33). This is the hope we want to share with those caught in the bondage of sin, including girls exploited and enslaved.

Tim Keller explains this concept of a broken tapestry in his book, *Generous Justice*. Keller writes,

> Because our relationship with God has broken down, shalom (peace and flourishing) is gone— spiritually, psychologically, socially, and

physically…. However, to 'do justice' means to go to the places where the fabric of shalom has broken down, where the weaker members of societies are falling through the fabric, and to repair it.[8]

This is the heart of Save Our Sisters. Our primary purpose in the mission of reaching Moldova is to bring Christ to the lost. We are seeking to restore the "shalom" of this society and aid as "ministers of reconciliation" to bring the hope of Jesus to this nation (2 Corinthians 5:17-21).

In the summer of 2011, Brianna and Morgan travelled to Cahul, Moldova. During their time there, they were blessed with the incredible opportunity to visit a Project Rescue Freedom Home, a safe house for rescued victims of trafficking in the capital city of Chisinau. This home is one of thirteen safe homes run by the missionaries of Project Rescue. From Morgan and Brianna's first greetings with the girls in the home, they immediately felt the love of Christ exude from the sweet spirits of these young survivors. The time in the Freedom Home not only brought them much joy, but also made them wonder, what about the rest of the victims?

Throughout the time in Cahul, Brianna and Morgan felt the increasing need for a safe home in that city because of the lack of safe shelter for victims. Located in southern Moldova, Cahul has a population hovering around 40,000.[9] This small, seemingly unimportant town is not exempt from the horror of sexual slavery. This fact, along with other personal testimonies, has confirmed our desire to mobilize godly change in the city of Cahul and its surrounding villages.

The Safe Home and the Local Church

Since that trip, Save Our Sisters has been pursuing the dream of building a safe home in Cahul, Moldova. To help us achieve this goal, SOS has partnered with an organization called Moldova Mission.[10] Moldova Mission consists of a board of multi-national Christian men passionate about bringing change to the country. This organization grew out of a local church partnership in Cahul, with Immanuel Baptist Church. Immanuel Baptist Church was planted by Christ Baptist Church of Raleigh, North Carolina seventeen years ago. Teaching and practicing the value of local church community is the heart of our ministry. The partnership between our home church in Winston-Salem, Christ Baptist in Raleigh, and Immanuel Baptist in Cahul, Moldova is such incredible evidence of the church acting as Christ's hands and feet, and we love to see the global partnership of local churches.

Morgan and McCall's uncle, Phil Medlin, husband to Aunt Linda who was at our first fundraiser for Save Our Sisters, serves as the Mission's Pastor of Christ Baptist Church in Raleigh, and has been traveling to Moldova since 2005. Having these established relationships in place years before SOS was even formed is one more example of God's sovereignty over the details—he continues to humble us with his sovereign plans.

Another pivotal member of Moldova Mission who has worked diligently to make this dream a reality is Anatol Dunas, the preaching pastor of Immanuel Baptist Church. He lives in Cahul, Moldova with his wife, Nadea, and their four sons. He and his wife have dedicated their entire lives to the Kingdom work of Christ. His life is a story of redemption and sacrifice. Their vision for this camp land project undoubtedly stems from their unwavering faith in the gospel, but also from their personal experience of human trafficking in their home country of Moldova. With close friends and members of their local church having endured the horrors of sex trafficking, Anatol and Nadea know the need for safe houses where at-risk children can find refuge, and rescued survivors can find restoration.

In joining with Moldova Mission, God has shown us how this project is bigger than SOS. The vision for this project includes a summer camp which will be used to spread the gospel to the people of the surrounding villages and cities, and two homes for vulnerable children that will provide shelter from the streets and prevention of trafficking through love, stability, and education. The camp land will also serve as a community center to be used year-round for pastoral training, retreat, and discipleship. There are also rooms available for victims of sex trafficking, should someone need a place to stay, and counseling from experienced believers in the local church to begin the restorative process. Over twenty-five acres of lush property encompass the buildings for this community restoration project. The summer camp has the potential to reach thousands of kids each summer which is an incredible opportunity for the gospel to go forth. Rescued girls in the SOS safe home will be able to work at the camp, providing a meaningful income opportunity to start their new life. Our prayer is that this place will be a haven of healing, hope, and flourishing. It is our joy to watch as God has sparked life into the hearts of this faith community as they fight against the economic and social enslavements of this struggling country.

Along with the faithful partners on the ground in Moldova, a board of American businessmen called The OAR Foundation have significantly contributed towards our mission. They have graciously managed all of our finances and offered us valuable wisdom in maintaining faithful ministry. This was especially important considering we were handling and transferring thousands of dollars from our fundraisers when we were fourteen years old.

The relationships we have formed with these wise mentors is an example of the church at large, working together for the glory of God. It has been incredible to see how multi-generational the work of Save Our Sisters has become, and we cannot thank the Lord enough for showing his grace by manifesting to us the Titus 2 passages about mentorship. In Titus 2:2-8, Paul is encouraging the older women to disciple the younger women and the older men to disciple the younger men, just as a family with godly parents would work. The leadership team of Save Our Sisters has experienced generational discipleship throughout our time working with the Moldova Mission project and for that we are eternally grateful.

Transformation by Gospel Grace

The vision for these restorative safe homes is for the glory of Christ to be magnified. It is our desire to make this a safe home where the girls can be exposed to the love of Christ demonstrated day in and day out through all relationships and in everything we do. Our dream is for this to be a home, not a three-month rehabilitation center, but a place where healing can begin—physically, emotionally, psychologically, and spiritually. We believe that if we have not shared with these girls the freedom that can be found in Christ, we have done nothing. True liberty and peace rests in him alone. It is our prayer that through their experience in the safe homes they will taste the unconditional love of a Christ-centered family where the gospel is on constant display.

Among other things, the girls living in the safe homes will be taught a vocational trade. Often rescued victims of the sex-trade find themselves returning to trafficking, due to lack of education and jobs skills. Selling their bodies is simply all they know, and all they feel they are capable of doing in order to make a living. By providing the girls an opportunity to learn a new occupation, we pray their lives may flourish. The property of the camp land beautifully lends itself to agricultural vocational training. The lush and fertile ground will be used to produce food, grow walnut trees, and raise honey bees, all of which will sustain the camp and be used for vocational discipleship.

In addition to the home, the land in Cahul will also be used for family camps, agricultural training, pastor training, and Bible school. The majority of the SOS leadership team members have served as counselors for the sports camp in Moldova over the years and can testify to this: church sports camps in Moldova serve as one of the main means of evangelism in the lives of unchurched Moldovan teens. Sadly, the current camp limits the amount of students who can attend camp each summer and hundreds of teens are turned away due to lack of space. However, the new Moldova Mission camp will allow plenty of space to serve students year round—a catalyst to share the gospel with as many teens as possible. With the space and availability at the Moldova Mission camp, there will be room to share the gospel with 160 students each week, for 7-12 weeks every summer! That is incredible potential for not only evangelism, but opportunity for one-on-one discipleship as well.

If you have caught the vision for Moldova Mission and desire to be involved, consider donating towards the final building costs of the camp, or give continually as a sponsor for a child in the Hope houses, or as a scholarship sponsor to send a student to camp! Learn more by visiting www.moldovamission.com

4

The American Reality

"This is the message we have heard from him and proclaim to you, that God is light, and in him there is no darkness at all."
1 John 1:5

It's Game Time

Adrenaline pumping. Fans screaming. It's seconds until kickoff. Traffickers have been preparing for weeks in advance, working on their own lineup for game day. The football game of the season has finally arrived, but with it comes hurt, pain, heartache, loneliness, and no chance of escape. On a Sunday in February, our nation gathers to watch the most anticipated sports event of the year. For most of us, this time is filled with food, commercials, and fellowship, but for thousands of girls nationwide, this weekend brings forth horror. Super Bowl weekend is one of the largest sources of sex-industry consumption in our country.[1] As a result of the large populations gathered for the game, the demand for sex-workers heightens. The Super Bowl, along with other major sporting events, is a magnet for sex trafficking and child prostitution. With many men looking to celebrate and have a good time away from their wives and families, the demand for sex workers in the Super Bowl host city increases. As horrifying as this was to learn in the midst of our trafficking research, we found that these types of situations are not uncommon.

The city of Charlotte, North Carolina is ranked first in the state and in the top ten cities with the highest percentage of trafficked victims in the US.[2] No matter how much we try to hide ourselves from reality, this issue is quickly rising to one of the top international crimes today. Sadly, America has become the primary consumer of trafficked victims around the world.[3] For example, because of the international airport, thousands of women are transported in and out of Atlanta, Georgia within days. Some trafficked women do not even leave the airport before they are transferred to another location for exploitation. We have heard story after story of successful businessmen leaving work slightly early to stop by a hotel room for thirty minutes to meet a victim before returning home to their families for dinner that night. Occasionally, an extended "business trip" to other countries will ensue. For up to weeks at a time, husbands, fathers, doctors, and lawyers will prance around a foreign country with a different girl on their arm each night, selfishly satisfying their sexual desires while destroying the lives of the trafficked. This trafficking trend is known as sex tourism.

International airport cities like Los Angeles, Atlanta, and Charlotte, to name a few, are major trafficking hot spots due to the international "cargo" coming from other countries. Many times trafficking victims will be sold and trafficked inside the airports to other traffickers who will transport them to many other regions of the country, without ever stepping foot outside. Due to the use of airports as a means of international transportation, flight attendants have made it a top priority to know the signs of trafficking and contact national authorities before the plane touches down if they are suspicious of trafficking activity. In 1996, Nancy Richard founded Airline Ambassadors, a non-profit organization that raises money and adopts charity causes through airline companies. One of their most recent projects made Human Trafficking Awareness Training available to all flight attendants through online training videos and weekend conferences.[4]

As a result of these training seminars, many flight attendants are now equipped and trained with how to respond to possible trafficking victims on their flights. There have been multiple trafficking arrests made in 2017 because flight attendants quickly recognized the signs of trafficking. One story belongs to Alaska Airlines attendant Shelia Fedrick, who noticed a girl with dirty hair and clothes traveling with a well-dressed business man who would not let the girl speak for herself, or make eye contact with Fedrick. Fedrick thought this was strange behavior and ended up leaving a note in the bathroom for the distressed girl who then responded asking for help. Fedrick contacted local authorities who met their flight at the terminal to investigate as soon as they touched down.[5]

Truck stops along highways are also known as trafficking hot-spots. This is another prominent form of transportation for trafficking victims, and the trade of victims happens at truck stops all over the United States. Sex dealers bring in women and girls from previous stops along busy highways to "work" yet another night.[6] Many truckers transit these stops every day to rest and can often satisfy their sexual appetite at the same location. Government agencies have noticed the connection between trafficking and truck stops and have partnered with truckers of integrity to form TAT: Truckers Against Trafficking.[7]

The culture of trafficking in America involves an unthinkable world of lies, leading young girls to believe that a prosperous life awaits them. Yet the face of trafficking takes on a sly ambition here in our own backyards. There is a whole world of underground brothels in the back of nail salons, and modeling jobs that make prostitution and pornography seem like a chosen lifestyle. These are just a few examples of how trafficking rears its head in the US.

Many times American victims come from broken homes where they have been abused, allowing their hunger for love, appreciation, and acceptance to make them extremely vulnerable. Traffickers prey on this type of victim, aware of their need for affirmation and self-worth. They know that these girls are longing to feel special and wanted. Many times pimps will send "scouters" into middle and high schools to befriend the next victim. These scouts can come in the form of a friend showing kindness, a flirtatious boy, or even older siblings breaking in the new victims.

Ashley and the 'Boyfriends'

Ashley was a sophomore in high school. She had just moved into town and hardly knew anyone but her teachers. She was never great at keeping relationships. Always a few pounds overweight with a constant pink complexion resembling that of a spring break sunburn, she was lonely but too shy to make friends in such a social battlefield. A couple weeks after school started, Maria began talking to Ashley, sitting with her at lunch and even complimenting her on her clothes. They giggled and joked and Ashley really enjoyed Maria's company.

One day Maria invited Ashley over for a sleepover on Friday night. Ashley went home excited and told her parents about the invitation. They were encouraged to see her making friends and enthusiastically agreed. Friday came, school ended, and the girls spoke of all the fun they would have that night. When they arrived at Maria's house she said her parents were out—this made Ashley a little nervous, but she ignored her gut feelings. They watched TV for a while and baked cookies, laughing the entire time.

It was getting dark and they went to the basement to watch a movie. About thirty minutes later there was a knock on the door. Maria jumped up to answer it and there were two older boys. Ashley recognized one of them, she had seen him pick Maria up from school before. The other one looked like he could have been twenty years old, his eyes were dark and a shaggy goatee crested his chin. They made their way back down to the basement and resumed the movie. Maria cuddled up on the couch in the arms of her friend, Grey, and it did not take long before they both lost interest in the movie and began making out.

Maria kept nagging Ashley that Chris, the second guy, was really nice and she should have fun while she could! "Come on Ash, it's just a kiss or two! Calm down and have some fun!" Ashley wanted to fit in, she was careful not to mess up the new friendship with Maria, so she obliged. Chris began kissing her neck and soon he was on top of her.

She awoke the next morning to traffic whooshing by,

the road fleeting from under the wheels of the van. "Where are we?" she asked, her voice shaking. "You're one of us now, we travel a lot. What happened last night is only the beginning, Ashley."

Ashley never saw her parents again. Chris and Grey began sneaking drugs into her food to dull her resistance against their friends and other customers. One day they slipped and gave her too much. She overdosed only three months into this new lifestyle. She shares a story much like countless other victims.[8]

Brainwashed

Not only are these "scouts" sent into school systems, but into work places, malls, parks, and any other area where there is a plethora of insecure women and girls. In these recruitment situations, traffickers and recruiters alike often use the "middle girl" tactic. Out of three women, they will ignore the beautiful one because she is used to the attention and would think nothing of it. Neither will they choose the ugly girl because compliments are rarely given to her, and she would become easily suspicious. Rather, they choose the "middle girl" because she will appreciate the attention, just like Ashley. Manipulation like this plagues the business world of trafficking. Once a vulnerable girl is under the control of a trafficker, she is stuck. No matter how hard she tries, she rarely ever gets out on her own. Often pimps use a trauma-bonding tactic to keep the victim within their grasp.[9]

With most of the girls coming from broken homes, the victims of this crime are often looking to find love and affection from someone, anyone, even if it comes with a price. Often men will start off the relationship as a "boyfriend" or "fiancé" figure in the girl's life, giving them jewelry, clothes, attention, and what seems to be love. In fear of losing their affection, these girls are willing to do almost anything for the men they believe truly care for them. After all, at this point the traffickers have provided some type of shelter and food for the victims, so losing these "boyfriends" would often mean losing everything. Traffickers are willing to buy very expensive gifts, but never directly give the girls the money they earned for their free use, keeping them absolutely dependent. It is estimated that one in every five American runaways reported to the National Center for Missing and Exploited Children are likely child sex trafficking victims.[10] The American foster care system can at times imitate international orphanages, where at the age of eighteen, children are no longer given education, shelter, and basic necessities but rather are turned out on their own to make a way for themselves. This often leaves American children vulnerable to anyone offering them the promise of a job, a home, or a family—whether or not those promises are valid. Traffickers prey on vulnerable children who have grown up in the foster care system and often call themselves "daddies" and likewise the victims "wifies" as a skewed representation of the family structure they are seeking.[11]

Many Americans are blind to the existence of slavery like this here in our own country. The rapidly progressing American society wants to turn a blind eye to the destitute forms of slavery in our land—especially with the African slave trade already a part of our nation's recent history. We have been raised in a culture that thinks of self before anything else, and what we don't like, we often pretend does not exist. This American environment makes it hard to believe that something so dehumanizing can happen daily in a country built on presupposed freedom. The reality of human sex trafficking prevalent in our cities, states, and country remains unseen and unnoticed by the public at large.

Participation and Responsibility

Most Americans are guilty of being unwitting participants in the entertainment culture that undoubtedly feeds into the cycle of trafficking. With the music we listen to, the words we use, and the entertainment we participate in, we are fueling the sex-slave industry by our consumption. A lenient sexual culture is encouraged by many of us, whether we realize it or not.

The daily consumption of our culture's media entertainment directly affects the demand for pornographic production. Music and movies today consist of derogatory messages continually set before us, slowly desensitizing our minds. The way that our culture depicts the worthlessness of women and girls encourages the objectification and commodifying manifested in sex trafficking. When words like "pimp," "whore," "sugar daddy," and "johns" are used among popular songs and even used with friends, we normalize and in some instances popularize the language of trafficking. Even if we choose not to acknowledge the facts, the language we use reflects the heart. Consider the entertainment choices you make and ask yourself if the content is honoring to God and his design for relationships and sexuality. People do not just wake up one day and decide to pimp out twelve girls, charging money in exchange for their sexuality. It is a slow acceptance to the degradation of sexual boundaries that leads to both the supply and demand of this industry.

Pornography

Do you want to do something about the global slavery epidemic? Stop watching pornography.

Pornography is inextricably linked to the international sex-slave trade. Nearly one-third of the women and children found in pornographic material have been forced, coerced or threated into preforming sex acts in front of cameras[12] and many of them are sold, traded and trafficked by pimps.[13] The connection between the sex-slave industry and pornography can no longer go unnoticed.

Cyber Sex Trafficking is one of the largest revenue contributors to the sex slave industry. The revenue from sex trafficking is higher than ever before at $99 billion dollars annually, and that is largely due to Internet consumers.[14] Many of the "modeling" jobs that traffickers use to lure women and girls into their business begins with traditional modeling but quickly escalates into the production of pornography. Traffickers will use threats against the models own life, or the lives of their families to get them to comply with taking pornographic photos and videos.

This material is then sold to porn sites and publications, directly contributing to the demand to act out these cyber fantasies in real physical form. President of the International Mission Board, David Platt, writes about the connection between sex trafficking and pornography in his book, *Counter Culture*. Platt writes,

> Another study on the relationship between prostitution, pornography, and trafficking found that one half of nearly nine hundred prostitutes in nine different countries reported pornography being made of them while in prostitution. When we hear such statistics, we must not miss the connection. Men and women who indulge in pornography are creating the demand for more

prostitutes, and in turn they are fueling the sex-trafficking industry.[15]

In addition to explicit pornography, the soft porn found in many movies and shows today are the result of America's hyper-sexualized culture and further desensitize us to the humanity of the person we are watching. A prime example of this is the outrageous success of the novel-made-movie, *50 Shades of Grey* by E. L. James, which brought in over $500 million dollars in global box office sales.[16] Sex sells—but only because it is in demand.

When God's good plan for sex is defiled, corruption occurs as we see in every aspect of sex trafficking. These victims have experienced such a dishonored view of sexuality. Purity and respect are almost entirely absent in our culture's depiction of marriage. And although marriage can be viewed as optional for many today, for believers, marriage is a beautiful covenant between one another and God. We are called to bring his purpose to the world not only in freeing these hopeless victims, but also by displaying the gospel in our own marriage relationships as we reflect the relationship between Christ and the church (Ephesians 5:31-33).

With such a massive issue at hand, it is easy to become overwhelmed at the amount of work to be done in the fight against human sex trafficking. But God does not command us to fix all of the world's problems, he simply commands us to love him first, and to love our neighbors as ourselves (Mark 12:30-31). Although the SOS ministry is not actively building a safe home in America, we are constantly engaged in education and advocacy against trafficking. Christ has intentionally placed us here, where we are, to advocate on behalf of our sisters by raising awareness and challenging the Church body to respond to this oppression, both domestically and internationally.

Learning more about trafficking has made our hearts heavy. The stories are sobering and difficult to think about but once we heard them we had to take action and encourage others to do so too. In order to act, you must first educate yourself. Get outside your comfort zone and be a light to those who are in the darkness. Learn the signs of trafficking in America and look out for suspicious activity.

Recognizing indicators of human trafficking is the first step in identifying victims and prosecuting perpetrators. Here is a small list of indicators from the Human Trafficking Hotline to keep in mind:

Common Work and Living Conditions
The individual(s) in question:
- Is not free to leave or come and go as he/she wishes
- Is under 18 and is providing commercial sex acts
- Is in the commercial sex industry and has a pimp
- Is unpaid, paid very little, or paid only through tips
- Works excessively long and/or unusual hours

- Is not allowed breaks or suffers under unusual restrictions at work
- Owes a large debt and is unable to pay it off
- Was recruited through false promises concerning the nature and conditions of his/her work
- High security measures exist in the work and/or living locations (e.g. opaque windows, boarded up windows, bars on windows, barbed wire, security cameras, etc.)

Poor Mental Health or Abnormal Behavior:
- Is fearful, anxious, depressed, submissive, tense, or nervous/paranoid
- Exhibits unusually fearful or anxious behavior after bringing up law enforcement
- Avoids eye contact and conversation

Poor Physical Health:
- Lacks health care
- Appears malnourished
- Shows signs of physical and/or sexual abuse, physical restraint, confinement, or torture

Lack of Control:
- Has few or no personal possessions
- Is not in control of his/her own money, no financial records, or bank account
- Is not in control of his/her own identification

documents (ID or passport)
- Is not allowed or able to speak for themselves (a third party may insist on being present and/or translating)

Other:
- Claims of just visiting and inability to clarify where he/she is staying
- Lack of knowledge of whereabouts and/or does not know what city he/she is in
- Lost sense of time
- Has numerous inconsistencies in his/her story

This list is not exhaustive and represents only a selection of possible indicators. If you want to learn more about human trafficking in America and how to look for the signs, visit www.humantrafficking-hotline.org.[17]

The face of slavery in America is often hidden, or takes on a covert mask. We must rise to fight against not only the trafficking of bodies, but our culture's enslavement to sexuality.

Reflect on this: How can you take a stand in your own life, saying "no" to what culture is selling you?

5

Freedom in Christ

"So if the Son sets you free, you will be free
indeed."
John 8:36

The Young Man and the Brothel Door

*"The young man who rings the bell at the brothel is
unconsciously looking for God."[1]*

How could this be?

Could this evil of injustice be of God?

*The young man at the brothel, what is his search? A
search for the deepest desires of the soul—FILLED.*

*How can the pimp be closer to truth than the
moralist? Because he seeks after the desire of his heart—
the God-given desire to experience and enjoy deep*

intimacy through Christ. Yet, he seeks in the wrong place.

The man searching for intimacy, for communion, for knowledge of another person, he wanders.

If the man has not found true intimacy in the marriage of Christ and His Bride, he seeks the answer, the stuffing of the heart's void, in anything he can find. The man is designed to passionately crave intimacy. Yet, when found in the wrong place, outside the Kingdom of God, whether in drugs, alcohol, materialism, work, power, or control (such as control of another person's sexuality), the void remains empty, as if nothing had attempted to fill it. In addition, the individuals misused trying to fill the void end up with innocence stripped from them and hearts broken.

Could the man at the brothel door be in search of GOD Himself? Unconsciously, as the man attempts to fill, to be filled, he fails. He searches for acceptance, for love. He feeds the need to experience something beyond this life, something glorious. Something like sex—intimacy in its truest form.

He seeks God, intimacy masked as sex.

A man's desire is a desire for God. For the Intimate. The only One who can satisfy the void.

The victims of human trafficking are the abused women and children, but could it be that the man is a victim also? A victim of false hope and failed fullness? A victim of void intimacy—intimacy without love and sacrifice is not intimacy at all. In the search for fullness, the deep need for intimacy, the victim-man needs Christ, the

Intimate One.

Let us join in prayer for the captors of the innocent. We are more alike than we'd ever dare to dream, because we are all enslaved to something.

Written by Brianna Copeland

How Can We Relate?

In the beginning months of this ministry, we found the statistics staggering. We learned so much and began to find ourselves wondering how we could relate to the brokenness of the victims. God began to break our hearts and reveal to us our own depraved state apart from him.

Coming to grips with the reality of trafficked women and their captors demands fighting for freedom with vigor, and letting our compassion be moved to action. This justice issue is greater than a human rights cause, rather, it is a gospel matter of utmost importance. As believers, our resonance with the trafficked lies deeper than surface humanitarian aid. While they are physical slaves to captors, sin binds us to a life of flesh and selfishness apart from Christ. Our fragile, feeble souls are held captive to self and captive to sin. As traffickers coerce and deceive young girls for carnal gain, likewise we manipulate others in a way that pleases our own end goal. In the same way that men buy these young girls for pleasure, we readily seek worldly things to fill the empty hole in our hearts. When it comes down to it, we are all enslaved to something in our lives. The lives of these girls provide a literal picture of slavery. Yet, if we dig a little bit deeper, we see places of bondage in each of our lives. Maleah's testimony of how Christ called her to the work of Save Our Sisters clearly displays this idea. Here's her story.

Maleah's Story

My sister, Brianna, began this project as a key leader since the beginning. I had the privilege of watching everything that was happening from the outside and how God was moving. As Brianna educated herself on this issue, the facts about trafficking and the horrific things that were occurring around us became a prominent topic in our home. Things were happening so fast, I could barely tell what was going on, but slowly I came to realize what my sister was doing and the evil she was fighting against. I read story after story of girls my age that had been taken captive by traffickers, and I began to struggle with the idea of helping these girls that seemed to be so different from me. I thought, "How am I supposed to relate to these girls and speak for them when I have absolutely no idea what they are going through? I have never experienced anything like what they experience every day and I have no clue how they feel." For a while, these thoughts captivated my mind and held me back from doing anything. But, praise the Lord, He is faithful and began to show me how similar I am to these girls. The

Lord showed me that I was once enslaved as well. Yes, I wasn't physically enslaved, but I was just as much a slave to myself, my sin, and the desires of my flesh as these girls are to their captors. God revealed this to me and began to place a burden on my heart to share this. I know what it is to be enslaved, but I also know what it is to be free. As much as we want to give these girls freedom from the traffickers and put them in a safe place, we know that they will never be truly free unless Christ frees them. We can house them and clothe them and feed them, but if we don't give them Jesus, what have we done for them? This is how God called me to fight for freedom.

> At one time we too were foolish, disobedient, deceived, and enslaved by all kinds of passions and pleasures. We lived in malice and envy, being hated and hating one another. But when the kindness and love of God our Savior appeared, He saved us, not because of righteous things we had done, but because of His mercy.
>
> Titus 3:3-5

Enslaved to Sin

We were made to worship. You've probably heard that before. From admiring creation, to obsessing over sports, to idolizing celebrities, our hearts are created to make much of the things we love. We constantly find things in our daily lives to delight in and enjoy. But here's the catch—our hearts are fallen, dark, and deceived. We forget God. We worship the created instead of the Creator (Romans 1:23). Because of sin, rather than ascribing God's worth back to him, we twist it to place good things onto the pedestal of ultimate things in our lives. Whenever an object of worship is threatened, we irrationally act out to protect our idols.

The problem is sin, and Christ stands as the only remedy. This problem goes all the way back to the Garden of Eden. When we rebelled against God's authority, we broke relationship with him. In choosing to make our own gods, chaos entered the world. The consequence of sin is death. Not only physical death but spiritual death and the death of order, peace, and harmony (Genesis 3). We were dead in our sins (Romans 3:23, Ephesians 2:1). We were enslaved to sin. The curse held us in bondage. We were powerless to save ourselves because everyone was born with a sin nature. We needed a redeemer.

No Longer Slaves

Our God does not forsake us. He didn't leave us to wallow and eternally drown in our transgressions. By God's grace, he sent his only Son, born of a virgin and born under the law, to redeem us from the law (Galatians 3:13). Jesus Christ took on flesh and walked the earth nearly two thousand years ago, fully God and fully man. Our Messiah thought his deity nothing to be grasped and humbly set aside his crown to seek and save the lost. The one by whom and through whom and to whom all things were created, came to serve the least of these. By his life, he showed us what holy love looks like, he restored to us the picture of the Triune community, making much of each other and never themselves.

His life was blameless. Never to sin, he was incandescently pure and entirely innocent. You would think everyone would want Jesus as a best friend, to love him and know him deeply. This was only true of a select few, the disciples. Many hated him, accusing him of false teaching.

We despised him—so much so that we demanded he stand before the counsel. His crime? Blasphemy.

Some called him 'king of the Jews' and mocked him. Pilate found him faultless and decided to let him go but the crowd would not have it. We shouted, "Crucify him!" and demanded Jesus be sentenced to death—death on a cross. And so he was led like a Lamb to the slaughter. All the weight of every sin was felt in his body, and he bore the full wrath of God. Though he pleaded for a way out, Christ submitted to the will of the Father and breathed his last.

But that was not the end. He was placed in a tomb, and three days later the tomb was found empty. No one stole the body, no animals devoured the corpse; Jesus

Christ was alive. With the final breath of Christ, justification for sinners was possible and the curse was reversed. God the Father raised Jesus up from the dead; the grave had no power over him. In Jesus's resurrection, death had died. He paid the debt in full. By calling on him and believing in his name we are free! Covered in the blood of Jesus we are made right with God—our relationship is restored!

This is the greatest news of human history! Our God has paid the price to redeem us! It doesn't stop there—he is making all things new. Replacing our heart of stone with a heart of flesh and opening our eyes to see his goodness, God calls us his children!

Jesus Christ is the answer. He is the answer to the injustice of slavery and the issues of our own hearts. Without him we are nothing, and we must continually seek his face. Through him, glorious hope, peace, and joy await. Freedom is found here.

This freedom gives us perseverance, because we know that the work of justice is not an easy task, but one requiring patient endurance. Matt Chandler reminds us that even in times of trying ministry we "are driven with gladness, not guilt, being ever reminded of our forgiveness in the gospel, not our failures in the law. It is God's ability, not ours. Again and again."[2] The continual encouragement and endurance of the gospel gives hope to believers, providing purpose to the work of justice.

Isaiah 61

Isaiah 61 has been the Scripture passage for our ministry since the very first night at the sleepover. At that point in our story, a few of our families were memorizing Isaiah 61:1-4 and it instantly came to mind at the mention of Save Our Sisters. We have fallen back on this passage time and time again, reveling in new thoughts and new findings as the Holy Spirit reveals more of God's heart to us.

This same passage of Scripture is found again in Luke 4, when Jesus is speaking in the synagogue. After forty days in the wilderness being tempted by the devil, Jesus makes his way into Galilee, by the power of the Spirit. His earthly ministry as the Son of God could fully begin.

Jesus came to Nazareth, the place of his childhood, and began sharing in the synagogue. He was handed a sacred scroll and found the place where it read:

> The Spirit of the Lord is on me, because he has anointed me to proclaim the good news to the poor. He has sent me to proclaim liberty to the captives and recovering of sight to the blind, to set at liberty the oppressed, to proclaim the year of the Lord's favor.
>
> Luke 4:18-19

After reading this passage, Jesus rolled up the scroll, handed it back to the attendant and said to the congregation, "Today, this prophecy has been fulfilled in your hearing" (Luke 4:21). Christ has fulfilled Isaiah's prophecies. Through his sinless life, sovereign death, and victorious resurrection Christ is making all things new. He has redeemed his bride, the Church, and all who call on his name will be saved.

Through Christ we are claiming these things as our own. For those of us who are in Christ, we have been anointed by the Spirit, we are now called to preach good news, to proclaim freedom for captives, to bind up the brokenhearted. The church is called to set captives free by proclaiming the gospel of Jesus Christ who died to save us. Jesus shall soon consume all things and redeem his kingdom from our fallen world. Until then, every believer is called to walk in justice because justice is a part of God's heart.

How will you respond?

All Things New

Christ must transform us, taking our heart of stone and waking us to fully live by daily dying to sin and self.

We know that our old self was crucified with him in order that the body of sin might be brought to nothing, so that we would no longer be enslaved to sin. For one who has died has been set free from sin. Now if we have died with Christ, we believe that we will also live with him. We know that Christ, being raised from the dead, will never die again; death no longer has dominion over him."

Romans 6:6-9

By God's grace we have been set free through the blood of the Lamb. We are no longer slaves to our sin, but slaves to righteousness in Christ! Now redeemed as children of God, we are citizens of a new world, and we have been given the opportunity to become an integral part of ushering in the kingdom of Christ here on earth. He is making all things new, restoring everything under the headship of Christ. We have been given the responsibility of returning to Christ as LORD, reconciling all things back to him who saved us.

> From now on, therefore, we regard no one according to the flesh. Even though we once regarded Christ according to the flesh, we regard him thus no longer. Therefore, if anyone is in Christ, he is a new creation. The old has passed away; behold, the new has come. All this is from God, who through Christ reconciled us to himself and gave us the ministry of reconciliation; that is, in Christ God was reconciling the world to himself, not counting their trespasses against them, and entrusting to us the message of reconciliation. Therefore, we are ambassadors for Christ, God making his appeal through us. We implore you on behalf of Christ, be reconciled to

God. For our sake he made him to be sin who knew no sin, so that in him we might become the righteousness of God.

2 Corinthians 5:16-21

So let us take action. We are ambassadors for Christ, representing Heaven and his majestic glory through which he shines his mercy, new every morning. When we represent Christ as his ambassadors, it means we are convinced that he is absolutely worth it. Why not live audaciously under the banner of Christ Jesus instead of being timid and reserved, afraid of what this world can do to us? Why not put aside the fleeting pleasures of this world and intentionally show someone the love that Christ has offered us? This call to carry the Good News to the nations—this responsibility to proclaim freedom and reconciliation—this is urgent. This dying world needs Jesus Christ.

As a reflection, ask yourself this: What brings about the greatest sense of urgency in my life?

Let it be Christ.

6

Faithfulness and the Future

"Let us hold fast to the confession of our hope
without wavering, for he who promised is faithful."
Hebrews 10:23

The Struggle

We never set out to start a ministry.

We just had a sleepover. But God placed in our lap the desire to act, and the call to be obedient. He has not stopped calling us, but has continued to give us more opportunities to walk in obedience. And just so you know, not all of this has been easy. We've cried many tears of discouragement and frustration with each other and the circumstances in which we have found ourselves. But God is always faithful. We know that the Lord will bring to completion what he began in Save Our Sisters (Philippians 1:6).

One of the hardest things we've encountered is how to lovingly respond to others in a Christ-exalting manner. Like we mentioned earlier, sharing in front of our youth group once paralyzed us. The realm of the unknown response we would receive from our peers absolutely scared us to death. Even though they graciously embraced the ideas we shared, the fear of man is still something we must repent of and ask the Lord to help us with every time we stand in front of an audience.

God gently refines us through each opportunity we have to process the response of others. We have had to learn how to respond to the occasional negative responses from those who question our work, or those who question the wisdom of our parents for letting us learn about so much evil. Our personal identities, and the identity of this ministry, rest in Christ alone, not in the opinions or comments of others. This is one of the struggles we have encountered, but he gives more grace (James 4:5).

A specific time of our refinement came through a "BBQ Bash" fundraiser we held in the summer of 2011, about a year after our first cook out event. We planned diligently leading up to this event, thinking that at this point we knew how to plan a successful fundraiser based on what God had done in the past. We were relying on our own abilities and expectations for what this day would hold, and it did not go as planned. We had prepared food expecting three hundred people, but once the rain started pouring, we were excited to see about fifty guests show up. Through rain and low attendance numbers, God used this specific fundraiser as a reminder of how he is in control of this ministry, from beginning to end, and we cannot do anything on our own.

We have realized that an important aspect of ministry is remembering God's goodness, and recognizing it as grace from his hand. When our hearts are aligned with Christ and we look to join God in where he is already working, miraculous things will unfold. His mercy often comes in ways we least expect.

Mary Clark's Story

One of the most encouraging responses we've experienced through SOS came in the form of a young abolitionist, Mary Clark. This spirited ten-year-old heard five minutes of our story in the form of zebra lined runways and funky dancing. In the Spring of 2012, SOS participated in a mother-daughter conference targeted towards 3rd-6th graders. Pink polka dots, zebra stripes, and daisies overtook our church in an event called Designed to Dazzle, led by mentor and friend, Mrs. Linda Kinney. As a part of the conference, the SOS members danced in a fashion show and shared a bit of our story on stage. Mary Clark listened in the audience that day, and the Lord burdened her heart to take action.

A few weeks later, we received a phone call from Mary Clark. She told us how she was planning on having a yard sale and giving all the proceeds to SOS. We were thrilled to hear her excitement and passion! Equipped with SOS brochures and lemonade for sale, Mary Clark worked the whole Saturday running the yard sale. Her sweet parents encouraged her the entire time, making sure everything was running smoothly.

The next month, SOS hosted a birthday party fundraiser on behalf of the voiceless. The purpose of this event was to remember all the children who, year after year, never get to celebrate their birthday because of their enslavement. The day was filled with laughter, smiles, cake, and a plethora of birthday party activities. Mary Clark had decided to give us her check from the yard sale at this special event, a birthday present to girls she would probably never meet. She presented us with a check for $700.00 dollars that day! To say the least, we were completely humbled by the bold faith of this fifth grader. Her passion has not stopped since then, writing letters and drawing pictures to display in the safe house someday. We consistently pray that the Lord will give us faith like a child!

Faithfully Mysterious

Another unexpected blessing came from a Southern Baptist church in Summerville, North Carolina. In July of 2012, SOS was given the opportunity to share our passion with Pleasant Garden Baptist Church. We received this invitation from the North Carolina Baptist State Evangelism Conference when we spoke with Dr. Alvin Reid, a professor at Southeastern Baptist Theological Seminary. Dr. Reid graciously allowed us to share an abridged version of our story with him on stage that March. Little did we know that this would multiply into two separate speaking engagements with two different churches in our state. One of those opportunities came from Pleasant Garden.

SOS was given around 20 minutes to share in all three services on a Sunday morning. We also spoke with the youth group as a means of kicking off their Vacation Bible School. We were greatly encouraged by our time with the congregation, but honestly didn't expect what God had in store. The church planned to donate all the funds they raised during the week of Vacation Bible School, but because of the unpredictability of VBS offerings we didn't expect much. Obviously this was not the right attitude for our hearts, doubting the good plans of our Father.

The following week, Morgan and McCall boarded a plane and traveled across the Atlantic to serve for ten days in Moldova. They returned with great passion and vision for the safe home project. Off the heels of such an incredible trip, our time spent at Pleasant Garden was not pressing hard on our minds. Little did we know that our lives would be changed by a generous congregation and passionate pastor who simply believed in the faithful work of God.

During Morgan and McCall's time in Moldova, they learned of the massive need to begin the grading process on the camp land. Without funds to proceed, the entire process stood at a standstill. Our immediate response was to gather together and pray with our families, determining whether we should send $6,000 to fund the grading. We felt the Spirit prompting us to step out in faith and send the check. Withdrawing $6,000 from our slender SOS savings would press us for intensive fundraising over the fall semester to replenish what we had sent. We felt the monetary burden, but we trusted that the Lord would not forsake us. All of the girls huddled outside on the porch, nodding in agreement that God was calling us to action. No sooner than we said amen, a full rainbow of promise stretched across the entire sky. A miracle, as it had not rained once all afternoon. Oh, how the Lord works in mysterious ways sometimes!

The Unexpected

The following day at our Sunday morning worship gathering we were approached by a sweet couple who have dedicated their lives to a similar mercy ministry involved with resettling refugees. Unexpectedly, they handed us a check for $1,000. They shared how they felt the Lord working in their hearts, urging them to give. That one thousand dollars has now been used to plant 217 trees all along the home property, providing vital shade and irrigation to the land. Isaiah 61 parallels so poignantly as it reads, "...that they may be called oaks of righteousness, a planting of the Lord, that he might be glorified" (Isaiah 61:3).

After all of that excitement, we were not sure that our hearts could handle anything else and yet, the following Wednesday morning we received a phone call from Michael Barrett, the pastor from Pleasant Garden. In the midst of our flurry of decisions, that speaking opportunity from a few weeks ago had somewhat faded to a memory, but we were excited to hear how God had moved through their VBS. We chatted for a bit and then nonchalantly pastor Barrett broke the news..."Oh and by the way, we are sending a $10,000 check for you in the mail today."

TEN THOUSAND DOLLARS!?!?

The phone hit the floor. Tears came quickly as Morgan attempted to formulate some sort of thank you to such astounding generosity. This was the single-largest donation that we had ever received for Save Our Sisters. The money was immediately put to use, and the grading project in Moldova was quickly completed! The thrill of breaking ground in Moldova, combined with enough funds to back it up, kept us on our toes for the next couple months! The Lord brought in eleven thousand dollars in four days. Sometimes the way the Lord mysteriously works is his way of leading us gently, and moving our hearts to wonder in awe of him.

Over the course of the next few weeks, we shared this miracle with nearly everyone we talked to. The radio, college professors, grocery store donors—you name it. This is one story too great to keep to ourselves! We were given the opportunity to recount this crazy grace at Southeastern Baptist Theological Seminary the next Thursday, where Dr. Reid invited us to speak in one of his classes, re-telling of God's mercy through our ministry. The five minutes that we shared with him on a stage in April led to one of the most unimaginable and unexpected gifts. How incredible it is to watch God weave circumstances together in such a beautiful tapestry only he could design.

7

Moved to Action

"Praying at all times in the Spirit, with all prayer and
supplication. To that end, keep alert with all
perseverance, making supplication for all the saints."
Ephesians 6:18

Prayer Works Miracles

SOS began with a simple prayer. Our honest cry was
for God to use us as vessels of mercy, ushering in his
kingdom. We bowed our hearts before God, and we
surrendered our plans to him. Without the guidance of
prayer in our lives, any work of our own returns void.
Prayer humbles us, reminding us of our state apart from
Christ—that we are powerless to accomplish anything
without dying to self and relying fully on the Holy Spirit to

move (John 15:4). The Lord has shown us time and time again the power of seeking his face.

During our first event on the soccer field in September 2010, we set aside a specific time dedicated to prayer, focusing on different facets of this international crime. It was such an incredible moment. Kristie remembers stepping foot on the field during the time of prayer, looking around at everyone on their knees pleading on behalf of the broken, and feeling the power of the Holy Spirit at work in that moment.

The next day, exhausted and still overwhelmed by the outcome of the cookout, we looked online and found breaking news stating that over 200 girls had been freed in the Philippines from a trafficking ring bust. This served as one more thing to confirm that God was propelling SOS forward in ways we could have never imagined.

Looking back over the last several years to that first night, we had absolutely no idea what God had in store. He has guided us, touched countless lives, and continually taught us the power of his Word. From the beginning, the one thing we knew was that through the Scriptures, God placed a specific call on our lives.

So often we try to justify our laziness and apathy by disqualifying ourselves from the Great Commission. We believe the lie that something so critical and weighty is surely only dependent upon pastors, church leaders, and Christian "radicals"—not for the youth. We seek to remove ourselves from the mission of God because at times it seems unending, and we seem unqualified. If this call to follow Christ was manageable on our own, we could go about our individual lives with ease, relying only upon our strength and wisdom. But when faced with a task that feels impossible, we must acknowledge our frailty. Without the Lord's love for us, the way he continues to seek our hearts and bring us back to him in faith, we would be nothing. Absolutely nothing. We are learning to delight in our weakness, for that is when Christ's power is made most evident in us (2 Corinthians 12:9).

Everyday Justice

There is nothing about us that makes us 'fit' or 'adequate' for this mission. The first step is to simply say, "Here I am, God, send me" (Isaiah 6:8). So many times the devil steps in and tells us we are not good enough or that we don't believe enough. Though it can be hard, taking the first step in faith is all it takes—the Lord meets us where we are and his grace is sufficient.

Like we have said before, walking in justice is the call of the Christian. Jesus is the full manifestation of God himself—the physical embodiment of God's heart and character in the flesh. As the embodiment of God, Jesus makes it clear by the life that he lived and the words that he spoke that justice is a part of who God is and it effects every part of a life lived in obedience to God. In light of this, those who are in Christ, seeking to live a life of obedience, must walk in justice. Jesus makes this particularly clear in a conversation with the Pharisees, where he calls them out for trying to live religiously, following rules they've made up, while completely ignoring the most important things God commands of us: justice, mercy, and faithfulness (Matthew 23:23). Obedient Christians must walk in obedience to God, and God has called every believer to live in justice, mercy, and faithfulness every day.

God has confirmed this calling through specific moments in each of our individual journeys. Here are a few personal stories from within our SOS team:

That moment when you have gone over the same English word thirty-five times with a Karenni refugee that has recently moved from a refugee camp in Thailand to America, and they finally remember how to pronounce it and tell you the meaning, that is the moment when God proves his faithfulness in the lives of all his children. That is the moment when you realize that you really are not with those refugees just to teach them English, but to teach them Jesus.

- Maleah Weir

It's the moment when it clicks. When everything that was lost and confused and hazy in life finally becomes clear. Clear like water. They can see, because they have found Love. The love of Christ, spoken through me to them so that Life is found. Life in Christ. Whether Africa, Trinidad, Guatemala, or North Carolina, that moment of being found is the same. It is the moment when someone is found by the One that can save them: Jesus. That moment is worth it.

-Elise Griffin

Deciding to travel across the globe to an unknown country is hard. Leaving the comfort of America for two weeks is not easy. When you make that decision and arrive at a place more beautiful than you could have ever expected, when you look into the dark brown eyes of a hurting African and see a beautiful child looking back at you, you realize that the child standing there is a child of the same God that you are. That moment right there, knowing that Christ lives in us both and we can share in his joy, that moment is worth every struggle along the way.

-Kristie Watkins

That moment when you are at a camp in Moldova and a young girl comes up to you, pinches your cheeks and calls you beautiful after only knowing you for a few days. That moment when you realize that God has made everything in its own way, beautiful. 'You are fearfully and wonderfully made.' That is the moment when you know that in his own time, God will once again restore his world to its beautiful purpose.

-McCall Barney

That moment when you live life with the gospel fully on display through the art of being alive, when Jesus is seen in everything you do. When you can speak Truth into the lives of people around you, caring for the eternity of their souls and how they know and understand the world in which they live and the God in Whose image they are created. The moment when things start to make sense, by the Spirit's revelation. Hope is seen in their eyes, and the glory of Jesus in that moment is so worth it.

-Brianna Copeland

That moment when you return to serve in the beloved country of Moldova and everything has changed. The luscious fields, once filled with gorgeous sunflowers, are now dead and the soil black as night. The campers hearts seem to mimic the soil, hardened to the freedom in the gospel they have not yet heard. You don't understand why God has placed you in this position, but as the week continues, hearts begin to soften. They hear of the grace Christ freely extends to all who believe. Rain begins to fall from the clouds. A picture of pure grace. That is the moment when you realize even when we are faithless, he is faithful. That moment when you realize, he is good.

- Morgan Barney

If you can take that first step of surrender, you won't ever be able to turn back. You won't ever want to. When we allow God to work in our lives, when we taste and see that the Lord really is as good as he says he is, there's no turning back—true life is found! (Psalm 34:8). It seems easier said than done, but we as Christians are called to love and serve no matter the cost. We have to put aside normalcy and live the radical, selfless life we are called to lead. If we can take one glimpse into someone else's life, entering into their problems and triumphs with love, we truly can make a difference in the world. We cannot do it for ourselves and our own glory, but for the glory of our God and for the eternity of his children!

Compassion Leads to Action

We believe that compassion is not compassion until it leads to action. Although we have talked about hard things, we cannot shy away. We cannot remain numb to the pain of others. We have to take the first step of faith. Being a part of SOS is not always easy. We have speaking engagements, events, planning, and honestly, with a leadership team of six teenage girls, we don't always get along perfectly. Yet, our little inconveniences fade away when we take the time to stop and think about all that God has accomplished. Looking back, we would not change anything. It has definitely been a long, hard road at times, but God has been there every step of the way and continues to teach us more about his heart as he lights our way.

The Future for SOS

Over the past seven years, the members of SOS have grown and changed in tremendous ways. Our personal goals, dreams, and hopes for the future are very different from one another. However, we join hearts in our love for God and our passion to love the world. Our unity in Christ will continue to bind us together for the rest of our lives, and that is such an incredible picture of the body of Christ!

When SOS began we all felt the same passion to advocate for the oppressed. God placed the same burden on all of our hearts for sexually enslaved victims. We still feel that urgent desire to give a voice to the voiceless all over the world. Members from our group have travelled to Moldova, Uganda, India, Trinidad, Spain, Argentina, Brazil, Guatemala, Canada, Thailand, and different communities around the US. Many of these trips and ministries have included more than one family member from our team.

The involvement of our families in SOS from the beginning has encouraged us to take our passion to the nations. How beautiful it has been for our families not only to accept our heart for missions but to join us in serving! We have been blessed with the opportunity to grow up in homes where living missionally is not a distant dream but a reality of our everyday life in the gospel.

Throughout the last seven years of SOS, God has shifted our individual passions and spoken direction into each of our separate lives, especially through this season of college. It has been such a joy to watch the Lord multiply the work of Save Our Sisters as we have gone on to separate college campuses with completely new opportunities for advocacy and justice seeking. To name a few, these new avenues include writing justice entries for The Intersect Project blog, as well as policy reports for Shared Justice. It has been a precious gift to let the Lord continue to refine our theology of justice and teach us how to live out our beliefs in our everyday lives. Through times of growth and transition, one thing has remained: our drive to serve others and make God known. Being a part of this ministry has provided opportunity after opportunity to preach the gospel, share our passion for justice, and show others how they can strive after similar goals of making God known.

> And we know that for those who love God all things work together for good, for those who are called according to his purpose.
>
> Romans 8:28

This is not the end of our story. This is only the beginning. It is with great delight and unbelievable joy that in the summer of 2017, a group of the Save Our Sisters leadership team was able to be in Moldova soon after the grand opening of the first safe home for at-risk children and rescued trafficking victims! The Lord has been incredibly gracious and has given us abundantly more than we ever dared to dream about through the journey of SOS. Being able to be on the ground, seeing with our own eyes the fruit of the Spirit's work in our lives is beyond our wildest ambitions, and it leaves us truly humbled. Thank you for being a part of this crazy journey with us!

Now that you are aware of the reality of trafficking that plagues our world, you are responsible. As one of our dearest mentors Flossie Castle once stated, "When we were ignorant, we were innocent. But now that we have knowledge, we have responsibility."

We are all called to be abolitionists. To abolish slavery to self, to sin, to the lies of culture, and to the low expectations of teenagers in this generation. Consider how the Lord can use you to further the gospel and to walk in justice daily.

The time for abolition is today.

AFTERWORD

"He has told you, O man, what is good; and what
does the LORD require of you but to do justice,
and to love kindness, and to walk humbly with your
God?"
Micah 6:8

My first exposure to modern-day slavery was during a
trip to Southeast Asia several years ago. I had heard
about the issue of human trafficking, but its seemingly
distant reality had yet to awaken me to really consider its
atrocity. That changed one Sunday morning when I
stepped out of a Tuk Tuk in the outskirts of Phnom Penh,
Cambodia.

Our tour guide, who served as an investigator for a
local Non-Government Organization, began to describe
our surroundings and the plight of the vulnerable living in
the community. He shared stories of children, even as
young as five years old, being pimped out at night for the
purpose of sexual exploitation, only to return home with
an unspoken expectation to continue on as if everything

was normal. Tragically, for many, that was their normal. The investigator continued on, subtly pointing out the presence of a few known pimps seated outside in the distance who were eyeing our movements. "Be careful not to take pictures in that direction," he instructed with a slight head nod, "so as not to raise suspicion."

I tried to take in all the sights. There were children everywhere. Some were laughing and joining in with the Sunday School class that was meeting on the street just outside a former brothel. Some were curious yet wary of the activities, bearing what appeared to be an outward display of an inward wound. One little girl stood out to me as she leaned against a wall on the corner, watching what was going on around her. She stood downtrodden with her arms crossed, wearing what looked to be pajamas. Even now as I write, tears flood my eyes and questions flood my mind. Was she being exploited? Did she know that our Heavenly Father created her in his image and loves her? It was a haunting sight.

Upon my return home, I began to prayerfully seek the Lord's guidance. I needed help to process all the things I had seen and heard abroad. That assistance, I knew, could only come through the lens of God's Word and the work of his Spirit. What was I supposed to do with all that I had heard and seen? The temptation to feel overwhelmed was real. One morning I sat at the piano with my Bible opened to the book of Isaiah. The words from the pages of chapters one and fifty-eight poured forth in sync with a melody as I attempted to capture the twirling emotions within me. It became a song of release and a prayer of conviction.

I hear Your voice as You call me out of comfort
To lose control for the glory of Your Name

I'm letting go of this self-centered thinking
Lord, I need Your help to walk as Your Word says,

Seek justice
Rescue the oppressed
Defend the orphan
and plead the widow's cause

I hear Your voice calling me to action
To not stand idle in this world of desperate need
I lift my hands offering my all to you
For Your Name and Your Renown
is the desire of my soul

Seek justice
Rescue the oppressed
Defend the orphan
and plead the widow's cause

Is not the fast You choose?
To go and feed the hungry
To be Your hands and feet to everyone around me
To care for the broken-hearted
Showing mercy to the least of these
So that Your great name will be praised!

Seek justice
Rescue the oppressed
Defend the orphan
and plead the widow's cause

Will you seek justice?
Rescue the oppressed?
Defend the orphan?
And plead the widow's cause?

The issue of human trafficking is not a new phenomenon. We can read about it in the book of Genesis, recalling the story of Joseph in chapter thirty-seven. Fueled by jealousy and hatred, Joseph's brothers stripped him of his robe and threw him into a pit. They then sold him for twenty shekels to a band of Ishmaelite's passing by. They bought him and trafficked him to Egypt. Once Joseph arrived there, a captain of Pharaoh's guard by the name of Potiphar paid to bring him into his home as a slave. Thankfully, the story does not end there. Instead, we observe God's sovereign purposes unfold as he eventually uses Joseph to preserve his people.

Although there is nothing new under the sun, we live in a period of history where the number of slaves today far exceeds the number of slaves during the course of the entire trans-Atlantic slave trade. As you have read in the preceding pages of this book, there is an ongoing problem of buying, selling, and abusing persons made in the image of their Creator. You have read an amazing story of God using a handful of teenagers to form an organization that seeks not only to raise awareness of the problem of human trafficking, but also works to create a place for rescue and restoration in the country of Moldova. The question remains: what will you do about it? How will you be involved?

When I was confronted with that question for the first time there were several thoughts and doubts that arose in my mind. I was not a lawyer, a social worker, a law enforcement officer, or any other professional seemingly suited to the task. I did not possess the skills or credentials that one would think was necessary to do something. What could I do to affect this global problem?

One of the organizations I had connected with during our time in Southeast Asia was the International Justice Mission. Through further reading of their work, I quickly learned and resonated with their belief that foundational to the work of justice is the work of prayer. I might not be professionally trained as a first responder but I could certainly pray.

The more educated I became on the issue of modern-day slavery, the more I discovered I could do something. Doing something has looked different alongside the ebb and flow of life's seasons and responsibilities. Some of the ways I have been able to get involved have varied from building awareness through speaking to churches, to providing respite in our home to survivors of domestic minor sex trafficking, lobbying members of congress for stronger legislation, utilizing social media platforms like blogging in order to share information, leading prayer gatherings, mentoring young adults, and teaching my own children about our great God of justice. With my own handful of teenagers living under our roof these days, a lot of my justice advocacy is found in the need to further disciple our own kids in what it means to be imitators of God as beloved children.

God is a God of justice who invites his people to be instruments of his righteousness until that glorious day when he returns. On that day, he will wipe away every tear. He will make all sad and evil things come undone. He will make all things new. Until that day arrives when we see him face to face, we can rest in the knowledge that the same power that raised Christ from the dead is at work within us. God empowers his people through the work of Jesus on the cross and the power of the Holy Spirit to proclaim liberty to the captives.

Everyone can do something. The question is, what will your something be?

Kimberly Merida
Wife, mother, musician
International Justice Mission Justice Advocate

APPENDIX: PASTORAL STAFF Q & A

In addition to the stories of encouragement and hope brought from faithful supporters, our pastors and church leaders have greatly shepherded us through this entire process. They patiently weathered our crazy ideas, believed in our dreams, and gave us a chance. The Lord has blessed us with their valuable wisdom and dedication to our ministry. We conducted a "Q&A" with a few of our pastors and church leaders and have included their responses to give you an idea of what went through the mind of our leaders as we began this great endeavor we call Save Our Sisters. We hope that these answers will shed some light and be an encouragement to you, knowing that you might not be the only one who thinks this is crazy. Enjoy their thoughts!

When we first approached you about SOS what were some of your honest, initial thoughts?

"As one of your pastors my initial response was a mix of joyful encouragement and one of concern. I was so excited to see that you were passionate about making a difference in the lives of hurting and abused girls. I have always thought we expect too little from our youth in church. At the same time we all hear the horror stories of people in other countries who prey on the good intentions of philanthropic groups and embezzle their money. From the small amount of time I have spent with each of you girls I wanted to make sure you were protected. But, at times I underestimated your wisdom and discernment."

— Matt, Executive Pastor

"When I first heard about SOS I was humbled by the faith of a band of teenagers who were exposed to an incredible injustice and knew that there was something you guys could do to make a difference. So many times global justice issues seem so far away, which make them easy to ignore or seem impossible to touch in any kind of meaningful way. But praise God for his Spirit who says to his children, "all things are possible through the strength of Christ!" (Phil. 4:13). When I think about God's purpose in establishing his church to be his hands and, I think SOS is a beautiful outpouring of this purpose."

— Alexandra, Local Missions and
Community Development Coordinator

"When the SOS team approached me with the idea of building the rescue home and how much it would cost I smiled to myself thinking what a great opportunity to watch God take such an overwhelming idea and use it to build the faith of some future missions leaders. I have always been encouraged to watch God open doors and to see the joy as we have tried to participate with you. It is always good to be able to offer advice and encouragement."

— Steve, Missions Pastor

"I was amazed at the depth of insight and research that you had done. When we first talked I remember thinking there is no way our church will go for this, but it is worth fighting this battle to affirm these girls' passion to make Christ known by seeking restoration in the broken places of the world! It didn't surprise me a bit that you were persistent and planning big, because this type of thing doesn't arise in the hearts of people who aren't already passionately pursuing God!"

— Steven, Student Pastor

"My first thoughts about SOS led me back to a book I had read called *Do Hard Things*. The idea of not challenging students to do more than they ever thought possible was convicting as an adult leader. The very concepts laid out in this book were being lived out by SOS. They saw a need that aligned with their passion and joined where God was working. As an adult I saw my role to come along side and enable them to pursue their passion in whatever way God would use me."

— Tom, Student Ministry Volunteer

How did you initially want to respond?

"Initially I wanted to make sure that you girls were protected and guided through this process. After talking with pastor Al Gilbert about it, I felt confident that you had the support you needed." — Matt

"Being an eternal optimist, I wanted to respond with a great big 'YOU GO GIRLS. YOU LET THE SPIRIT USE YOU!' I know God's pattern in using the most unassuming folks to accomplish his mission so that he gets the glory. When you look at Scripture, you see that God so commonly uses the young, the weak, the people who don't make sense to bring about his purposes. I don't say this to say that you all are weak, but what I am saying is that for all the educated and seminary-trained folks that are a part of our church family, it's just like God to use a group of faith-filled teenagers to open the eyes and the heart of our church to the issue of human trafficking and give people such simple ways to respond. We boast in the Lord, and he gets all the glory!" — Alexandra

"I have made it one of my deepest passions to help students know that they have a role in the Body of Christ now, and although I had watched great ideas fail before, I can never stop affirming the vision that students are given by God to lead the Body into great things for the glory of God! Though subtle doubts loomed in my mind, I always wanted, hoped for, and prayed for great things to be seen of God through the vision of Save Our Sisters!" — Steven

What has been the most encouraging, frustrating, or challenging part of your involvement with SOS?

"The most encouraging thing about SOS has been the overall success of the effort. I believe that your efforts are making a true impact on individual's lives that will have implications for eternity. It is very rare that we find a group of students in the church who are not only passionate about helping others, but also have the persistence to make it happen. It is amazing to think that one conversation at a sleepover could launch a movement that effects a global humanitarian issue." — Matt

"My frustration for you guys was having to navigate church politics and policies in order to host a number of your events. I know why we have many of those policies in place, but I also know it can be frustrating to work within those bounds when you feel like they stifle the ministry that God has called you to do. Ministry is hard and requires faith. You have to put yourself and this "ministry baby" out in front of people and trust God with the results. There were moments when I felt the vulnerability of the ministry and wanted to guard you guys from the disappointment of unmet expectations or of people not being as passionate about this justice issue and SOS."

— Alexandra

"SOS's mission to rescue girls from sex trafficking, and especially focusing in Moldova, has been the most encouraging thing to see. A cause that hit close to them and is so prevalent needed attention. Through SOS's involvement, the problem of the sex trade is something our church and our community have become aware of, and because of SOS people have an opportunity to do something about it. The other thing I love about SOS is their creativity. The way they have raised awareness and funds is so unique and fresh. Through selling scarves, jewelry, cookie dough, and other things, they not only are raising money but awareness. As students, they have a great sense of 'marketing' and the importance of it."

— Tom

"The most encouraging thing about SOS has been watching the way you girls have handled with such humility this massive moving of God in so many people and places. You are always quick to see yourselves as reflectors of the greatness of God! The most challenging experience has been convincing a mega church staff and its congregation of the significance, authenticity, and legitimacy of this vision."

— Steven

Watching where God has taken this project, what are your thoughts towards SOS today and for the future?

"Remain steadfast. It takes time to get a movement off the ground. As you girls get older and travel to college your connections and network will expand. As that happens continue to cast vision for SOS. There are not many Christ-centered groups like yours that have a single-minded focus towards this terrible issue of sex trafficking."

— Matt

"I'm thrilled to think where God will take this ministry in the future. I think practically the tangible goal of building a Safe House in Moldova is exciting and gives you a goal to work towards; to know that the money that God is raising is not just going to random ministries (although that is not a bad thing), but that it's going to support the construction and ministry of a very real house that will meet the holistic needs of real girls coming out of the atrocities of human trafficking. I love the practical goal of seeing this house constructed and praying about the lives that will be changed as Christians offer physical and spiritual hope and healing. I think you all have established a great platform to not only educate others about this issue, but also inspire others to be used for redemptive purposes in a whole host of other issues related to brokenness."

— Alexandra

"As you continue to work towards your goal, I continue to see God strongly at work and encourage you to take things one step at a time believing that '...he who began a good work in you will bring it to completion.'"

— Steve

"My prayer for SOS in the future is that you stay the course as long as this is where God would have you to be. We live in a microwave society, and we have been sold the myth that everything can be resolved quickly. My prayer is for continued passion and patience and to see the plans God has revealed to you come to fruition. But beyond that, my prayer is that you would pass your passion onto younger students who would in turn catch a vision for where God is working and to do something, anything, to join him. I know the time will come when the core group will go your separate ways and my prayer is that because of how you have seen God work in your efforts of SOS, that you will be challenged to do bigger and greater things for God." — Tom

"My thoughts today about SOS are that God never ceases to amaze me. It is his faithfulness to bring to completion his good works that excites me about the future of SOS, after all this is only the beginning. I am convinced that SOS will become one of the foremost examples of how obedience to God and serving as he has equipped, no matter one's age or stage of life, results in nothing less than the great visibility of his glory among the nations! I believe that we will see this movement inspire many and prayerfully reach even more for the gospel!"

— Steven

What is your advice to us as we continue to seek God's plan and purpose?

"Keep the mission the mission. As your influence grows and your network spreads, beware of the draw towards personal renown. Your close relationships with one another in SOS are your greatest strength and your greatest weakness. Pray for each other continually. Seek reconciliation quickly. And run to the cross together. Marvel at the empty tomb together. I am so thankful for you girls and pray that God would continue to bless SOS."

— Matt

"I would first remind you that the same sin that causes humans to take advantage of others in such horrific ways as human trafficking is the same sin that separates you from God apart from the reconciliation and redemption that you have found in Christ. Consistently remind yourself as individuals and as a group of just how holy God is, just how atrocious sin is, and just how sweet the redemption is that is offered in Christ. Meditate on how God has graciously justified you and is in the process of sanctifying you. This is so important because it humbles us and gives us great hope. It gives us great compassion for both the abused and the abuser. I would say continue to walk in great faith praying and believing that ALL THINGS ARE POSSIBLE THROUGH CHRIST WHO GIVES YOU STRENGTH. At the same time, I would encourage you to hold the ministry loosely knowing that God's plan for SOS may be different than your plans. He may want to make it an international ministry that lives on for decades, or he may say that it was for a season to accomplish the task of building this one home in Moldova, which would be an incredible result of your faithful service. Along those lines, I would encourage you to be in prayer now about the direction of the ministry knowing that you all are going to college in the next several years and will probably be in different places, states, etc." — Alexandra

"My greatest advice is never stop being inspired by the grace God has shown you in Jesus Christ. This is where a heart of compassion MUST begin. May the things that you have heard and seen continually point you back to your Savior and may the gospel, which has first changed each of you girls, and will transform the hearts of many!"

— Steven

TAKE ACTION

You can make the choice to take action *today* in response to the information you have learned, but more importantly in response to God's heart for justice. Consider these action steps and how the Lord is calling your compassion into action:

1. Pray.

Pray for the issue of human trafficking and for slaves to be set free. Pray for the consumers who exploit and buy human beings time and time again, whether that be through a physical sexual encounter or pornographic material. Pray also for those who transport and traffick victims. Pray for the rescue of victims and the rehabilitation of survivors through the endless work of organizations and agencies pushing back the darkness of injustice. Pray for Christ to come again and restore all things.

2. Educate.

Educate your church, family, and others on the issue. Information can lead to action. See the Resources list on the following pages to learn how you can educate yourself about the issue of human trafficking.

3. Donate.

Prayerfully consider supporting Save Our Sisters. You can find out more about our ministry and learn how to give by visiting www.saveoursisterstoday.com.

4. Buy This Book.

Provide copies of this book to friends, families, youth groups, and others. This book is a great way to introduce people to the issue of human trafficking, social justice, and how every believer can be involved. You can order copies of the book here: www.saveoursisterstoday.com/our-book/

5. Buy Fair Trade.

Many survivors of sex trafficking learn a creative trade as a new means of supporting themselves. Buying goods and materials made by survivors is a great way to promote Fair Trade companies and support survivors in their new vocation. You can find Fair Trade goods from companies such as Freeset, Malia Designs, Nightlight Designs, iSanctuary, and Eden Jewelry, to name just a few.

6. Organize a Fundraiser.

Consider ways you can fundraise! Remember, Save Our Sisters started with a youth group cookout. Consider how you can organize and execute your own fundraiser. Visit our website to download the "Host Your Own Event" pdf. Here's the link! www.saveoursisterstoday.com/whats-the-problem

7. Share Your Passion.

We believe the best way to advocate for justice issues is to honestly share your passion! Let everyone know that you are passionate about justice because of the way the gospel has motivated you. The best way for others to know what you care about is to hear you talk about it— don't be afraid to share!

He has told you, o man, what is good;
And what does the LORD require of you
But to do justice, and to love kindness,
And to walk humbly with your God?
Micah 6:8

RESOURCES

In relation to sexual slavery, the best way to aid in eradicating this crime is to expose it. Educate yourself on the issue. By educating yourself, you gain responsibility for the information you learn, and a heightened awareness of the real world around you. Second only to prayer—we believe education is the most effective way to abolish slavery today because this is something everyone can do. Talk about it, don't hide it or hide from it. Then share what you learn with others so they are accountable to this new knowledge also. There is power in knowledge, and like the cliché, there is much bliss in ignorance—but not at the expense of thousands of captive and exploited lives. The issue of human trafficking is worth your attention.

Here are a few links to different organizations and resources to begin your education about the slave trade:

www.saveoursisterstoday.com

www.moldovamission.com

www.ijm.org

www.notforsalecampaign.org

www.thea21campaign.org

www.enditmovement.com

www.projectrescue.com

Books:

The Justice Calling by Bethany Hanke Hoang and Kristen Deede Johnson

Counter Culture by David Platt

Ordinary by Tony Merida

Behind the Soiled Curtain by David and Beth Grant

Priceless by Tom Davis

Undaunted by Christine Caine

From Congress to the Brothel by Linda Smith

The White Umbrella by Mary Francis Bowley

The Locust Effect by Gary Haugen

The Good News About Injustice by Gary Haugen

Just Courage by Gary Haugen

The Just Church by Jim Martin

***Documentaries and Movies:

Trade of Innocents

Nefarious

Taken

Whistleblower

Slumdog Millionaire

***Many of the documentaries about human trafficking are far too graphic to outweigh the benefit of the information they portray. What we put before our eyes matters, and in this case if you are blessed enough to never have to see what trafficking looks like, be thankful for that and instead of watching things you can never un-see, consider reading a helpful book or news story. When watching documentaries, view them with caution and a guarded heart.

ABOUT THE AUTHORS

Morgan Barney

Morgan Barney is a senior at Covenant College in Georgia, pursuing her undergraduate degree in International Studies. Since a young age, advocating for justice has been the root of many of her passions. Pursuing justice led Morgan to participate in other avenues of justice reform, such as co-authoring a policy report for the Center for Public Justice. Morgan desires to continue to walk in justice as she completes her education with hopes of working for a non-profit or government organization.

McCall Barney

McCall Barney is currently earning her Bachelor's degree in Nursing from Belmont University. She actively participates in her local church, serves alongside her university, and lives a life of welcoming others into her story. Since the beginning of SOS, McCall has blessed our ministry with attention to detail and organization in order to promote the overall wellbeing of the ministry. McCall walks in justice daily by not only loving her immediate community in Nashville, TN, but by serving others through her health care passion she works as summer camp nurse in Raleigh, NC.

Brianna Weir Copeland

Brianna is a senior at the College at Southeastern Baptist Theological Seminary in Wake Forest, NC with her husband, Travis. She will graduate with a BA in English and Christian Studies with the desire to use her passion for words to edify the church and share the gospel through writing. Brianna is continually learning about what it means to walk in justice as a reflection of who the Lord is and how his heart for justice should intersect with every area of life. You can find more about her and her writing at the intersectproject.org and briannacopeland.wordpress.com.

Elise Moore Griffin

Elise is currently living in Columbus, GA with her husband, Jonathan. Elise is seeking to further God's Kingdom by allowing the gospel to go forth in her everyday life as a full-time professional. Elise seeks justice by managing her business with ethical integrity and genuine love for her customers. Elise is eagerly waiting for God to show her what her next avenue of justice work is, whether that be in the domestic business world, or in world missions.

Kristie Watkins

Kristie Watkins is finishing her degree in Journalism and International Studies at Western Carolina University in Cullowhee, NC. After college, she desires to follow her call to see and love those who are unseen or tossed aside by society by combining that with her love for writing. She currently seeks justice daily by advocating for adoption and foster care by pouring into people in her life who are walking through seasons of trial.

Maleah Weir

Maleah is a student at the University of North Carolina in Asheville but is currently living in Southeast Asia as a Vocational Training intern for Wipe Every Tear Ministries. Through this internship, Maleah is doing exactly what she desires to do as a career, by combining her passion for art with the healing power of the gospel. Maleah is studying studio art and psychology and she dreams of incorporating art therapy into the lives of survivors of sex trafficking once she graduates.

To request one or more members of Save Our Sisters to come speak to your church, youth group, or ministry, contact us: info@saveoursisterstoday.com

ENDNOTES

FOREWARD
[1] Global Slavery Index 2016.
http://assets.globalslaveryindex.org/downloads/Global+Slavery+Index+2016.pdf

INTRODUCTION
[1] John Piper. *Don't Waste Your Life*. Wheaton, IL: 2003.

CHAPTER 1: THE SLAVE TRADE
[1] Often in European countries, when children age out of the orphan care systems, sometime at age 16 and sometimes 18, they are given the equivalent of about forty US dollars and a bus ticket. This is all they are provided with and expected to make a new life for themselves. Many traffickers wait at bus stations looking to prey on these children, appearing alone, insecure, and lost.
[2] United Nations International Children's Emergency Fund (UNICEF) Report 2015.
https://www.unicef.org/publications/files/UNICEF_Annual_Repo

rt_2015_En.pdf.

[3] Trafficking In Persons Report 2013.
https://www.state.gov/documents/organization/210737.pdf).

[4] Trafficking In Persons Report 2013.
https://www.state.gov/documents/organization/210737.pdf

[5] Global Slavery Index 2016.
http://assets.globalslaveryindex.org/downloads/Global+Slavery
+Index+2016.pdf.

[6] United Nations International Children's Emergency Fund
(UNICEF). 23 Sept 2010.
http://www.unicef.org/protection/index_exploitation.html.

[7] UNODC Report 2014. Figure 10, p 31.
http://www.unodc.org/documents/data-and ---
analysis/glotip/GLOTIP_2014_full_report.pdf.

[8] Jeremy Haken. Transnational Crime in the Developing
World. 2010. Global Financial Integrity.
http://www.gfintegrity.org/storage/gfip/documents/reports/tran
scrime/gfi_transnational_crime_web.pdf.

[9] Alexandra Sims. "Woman 'raped 43,000 times' speaks out
about Mexico's human trafficking rings." *Independent.* 11
November 2015.
http://www.independent.co.uk/news/world/americas/woman-
raped-43200-times-speaks-out-about-mexicos-human-
trafficking-rings-a6730436.html.

[10] It is noted that, "The average annual profits generated
by each woman in forced sexual servitude ($100,000) is
estimated to be five times more than the average profits
generated by labor trafficking victims worldwide ($21,800),
according to the Organization for Security and Co-operation in
Europe." OSCE Office of the Special Representative and
Coordinator for Combating Trafficking in Human Beings, 2010,

p 25.

[11] International Labor Organization 2014. *Profits and Poverty: The Economics of Forced Labour.* www.ilo.org/wcmsp5/groups/public/---ed_norm/--declaration/documents/publication/wcms_243391.pdf.

CHAPTER 2: THE STORY OF SAVE OUR SISTERS

[1] Nancy Leigh DeMoss and Dannah Gresh. *Lies Young Women Believe.* Chicago: Moody Publishers, 2008.

[2] UNODC Report 2014. Figure 10, p 31. http://www.unodc.org/documents/data-and ---analysis/glotip/GLOTIP_2014_full_report.pdf.

[3] Project Rescue exists to "rescue and restore victims of sexual slavery through the love and power of Jesus Christ. To learn more about the holistic work that Project Rescue does day in and day out, visit www.projectrescue.com.

[4] The International Justice Mission is a D.C. based non-profit organization that works ceaselessly to push back darkness at its core and protect the most vulnerable of societies all over the world. IJM partners with those working in local justice systems to help victims of violence through recue, restoration, restraint, and representation. As members of the IJM walk through this process with victims, they identify weaknesses in the justice system and help to make it stronger in order to protect the poor and limit violence in their country. To learn more about the work of the International Justice Mission visit their website here: www.ijm.org.

CHAPTER 3: SLAVERY IN MOLDOVA

[1] Global Slavery Index 2016.
www.globalslaveryindex.org/index/.

[2] Moldova Mission, www.moldovamission.org.

[3] Global Slavery Index 2016.
www.globalslaveryindex.org/index/.

[4] www.moldovamission.com

[5] Moldovan independence was officially recognized on
March 2, 1992, when Moldova gained membership to the
United Nations. The nation declared its own independence from
the Soviet Union in 1991 and was the co-founder of the post-
Soviet Commonwealth of Independent States.

[6] Migration Policy Institute 2003.
http://www.migrationpolicy.org/article/moldova-seeks-stability-
amid-mass-emigration.

[7] "Not all institutionalized children were orphans; the
number of children entrusted to the Government by needy
parents or by parents leaving the country in search of work,
reportedly was growing. NGOs estimated that up to 30,000
children were in institutions or foster homes. Due to lack of
funding, children's institutions had major problems including
inadequate food, "warehousing" of children, lack of heat in the
winter, and disease. U.S. Department of State. Country Reports
on Human Rights Practices. Bureau of Democracy, Human
Rights, and Labor 2003.
https://www.state.gov/j/drl/rls/hrrpt/2003/27854.htm.

[8] Tim Keller. Generous Justice: How God's Grace makes Us
Just. New York: Penguin Books, 2010.

[9] City Population 2014
https://www.citypopulation.de/Moldova.html.

[10] Moldova Mission is a multi-national NGO comprised of a
leadership board with representatives from multiple countries all

working together to see the hope of the gospel of Jesus Christ transform the lives of Moldovan children through the specific building project of a new camp land and all the ministry that will take place in Moldova as a result. To learn more about Moldova Mission, visit their website at www.moldovamission.com.

CHAPTER 4: THE AMERICAN REALITY

[1] Psychology Today, http://psychologytoday.com/blog/modern-day-slavery/201702/the-super-bowl-and-sex-trafficking

[2] "Human trafficking more likely as Charlotte region grows, authorities say." The Charlotte Observer. January 11, 2016. http://www.charlotteobserver.com/news/local/crime/article5415 3290.html.

[3] United Nations Office on Drugs and Crime. "Global Report on trafficking in Persons 2014. p 70. http://www.unodc.org/documents/data-and-analysis/glotip/GLOTIP_2014_full_report.pdf.

[4] Airline Ambassadors international, www.airlineamb.org.

[5] Maryse Gooden. "Alaska flight attendant praised for reportedly saving a human trafficking victim." Fox News. Fen 7, 2017. http://www.foxnews.com/travel/2017/02/07/alaska-flight-attendant-praised-for-reportedly-saving-human-trafficking-victim.html.

[6] "Sex Trafficking at Truck Stops At-A-Glance," *Polaris Project*, 2012. https://humantraffickinghotline.org/sites/default/files/Sex%20Trafficking%20at%20Truck%20Stops%20AAG.pdf.

[7] www.truckersagainsttrafficking.org

[8] Eryka Washington. "Survivor of Sex Trafficking Shares her

Harrowing Story with News 6." News 6 Orlando, Florida. Sept 20, 2016. http://www.clickorlando.com/news/investigators/survivor-of-sex-trafficking-shares-her-harrowing-story.

[9] Traumatic bonding is defined by strong emotional ties that develop between two persons where one person intermittently harasses, beats, threatens, abuses, or intimidates the other. For more information about this intriguing relationship visit Psych Central – Trauma Bonding. https://pro.psychcentral.com/recovery-expert/2015/10/what-is-trauma-bonding/.

[10] Polaris Project, 2017. https://polarisproject.org/facts.

[11] CAS Research and Education. "Foster care and human trafficking." http://www.casre.org/our_children/fcht/.

[12] Donna M Hughes, "The Demand for Victims of Sex Trafficking," Women's Studies Program, University of Rhode Island, June 2005, p 26. www.uri.edu/artsci/wms/hughes/demand_for_victims.pdf.

[13] M Farley. "Renting an Organ for Ten Minutes: What Tricks Tell us about Prostitution, Pornography, and Trafficking." 2007.

[14] International Labor Organization 2014. *Profits and Poverty: The Economics of Forced Labour.* www.ilo.org/wcmsp5/groups/public/---ed_norm/--declaration/documents/publication/wcms_243391.pdf.

[15] David Platt, Counter Culture. Carol Stream, IL: Tyndale House Publishing, 2015. p 123.

[16] Ben Child. "Fifty Shades of Grey Hits over $500 million at the global box office" The Guardian. March 6 2015. https://www.theguardian.com/film/2015/mar/06/fifty-shades-of-grey-hits-500-million-at-the-global-box-office.

[17] National Human Trafficking Hotline, Recognizing the Signs. If you think you have noticed signs of a human trafficking victim, call the National Hotline Number 1-888-373-7888. https://humantraffickinghotline.org/what-human-trafficking/recognizing-signs.

CHAPTER 5: FREEDOM IN CHRIST

[1] Bruce Marshall. *The World, the Flesh and Father Smith.* Boston: Houghton Mifflin Company, 1945.

[2] Matt Chandler. *Creature of the Word: The Jesus-Centered Church.* Nashville, TN: B&H Books, 1st edition, 2012.

Made in the USA
Middletown, DE
10 August 2017